RECORDED VERSIONS GUITAR

AUTHENTIC TRANSCRIPTIONS
WITH NOTES AND TABLATURE

Best ACOUSTIC GUITAR Son...

ISBN-13: 978-1-4234-1847-4

HAL•LEONARD® CORPORATION

7777 W. BLUEMOUND RD. P.O. BOX 13819 MILWAUKEE, WI 53213

Visit Hal Leonard Online at
www.halleonard.com

CONTENTS

4 ACROSS THE UNIVERSE
The Beatles

7 AGAINST THE WIND
Bob Seger & The Silver Bullet Band

16 ANGIE
The Rolling Stones

26 BABE, I'M GONNA LEAVE YOU
Led Zeppelin

39 BEHIND BLUE EYES
The Who

46 BREAKING THE GIRL
Red Hot Chili Peppers

48 CRAZY ON YOU
Heart

57 DAUGHTER
Pearl Jam

66 DISARM
Smashing Pumpkins

71 DUST IN THE WIND
Kansas

74 EVERY ROSE HAS ITS THORN
Poison

83 FOOLIN'
Def Leppard

89 FREE FALLIN'
Tom Petty

92 HAVE YOU EVER SEEN THE RAIN?
Creedence Clearwater Revival

96 HEAVEN BESIDE YOU
Alice in Chains

101 I'D LOVE TO CHANGE THE WORLD
Ten Years After

108 IRIS
Goo Goo Dolls

116 JANE SAYS
Jane's Addiction

120 THE JOKER
Steve Miller Band

135 LANDSLIDE
Fleetwood Mac

142 LIKE THE WAY I DO
Melissa Etheridge

153 LOVE THE ONE YOU'RE WITH
Stephen Stills

157 MAGGIE MAY
Rod Stewart

165 MELISSA
The Allman Brothers Band

172 MORE THAN WORDS
Extreme

180 NORWEGIAN WOOD
(THIS BIRD HAS FLOWN)
The Beatles

187 PINK HOUSES
John Mellencamp

196 SIGNS
Tesla

201 SILENT LUCIDITY
Queensryche

208 THE SPACE BETWEEN
Dave Matthews Band

212 TEARS IN HEAVEN
Eric Clapton

217 THICK AS A BRICK
Jethro Tull

228 UPSIDE DOWN
Jack Johnson

235 WANTED DEAD OR ALIVE
Bon Jovi

242 YOU'VE GOT A FRIEND
James Taylor

254 *Guitar Notation Legend*

Across the Universe

Words and Music by John Lennon and Paul McCartney

Noth-ing's gon-na change my world. ___

Noth-ing's gon-na change my world. ___ Noth-ing's gon-na change my world._

Verse

To Coda

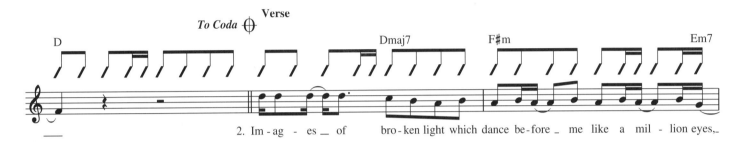

2. Im-ag-es ___ of bro-ken light which dance be-fore ___ me like a mil-lion eyes,_

___ they call me on and on ___ a-cross ___ the un-i - verse. _

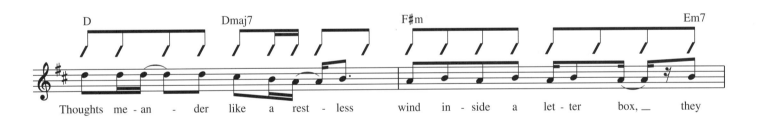

Thoughts me-an - der like a rest-less wind in-side a let-ter box, ___ they

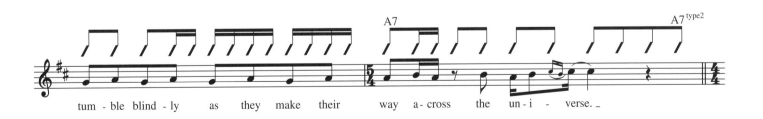

tum-ble blind-ly as they make their way a-cross the un-i - verse. _

Chorus

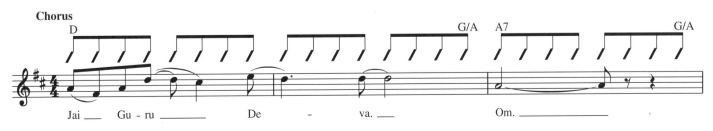

Jai ___ Gu - ru De - va. ___ Om. _____

Noth - ing's gon - na change my world. ___ Noth - ing's gon - na change my world. ___

___ Noth - ing's gon - na change my world. ___

Noth - ing's gon - na change my world. ___ 3. Sounds of laugh - ter, shades of life are

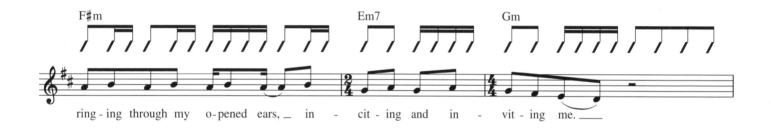

ring - ing through my o - pened ears, _ in - cit - ing and in - vit - ing me. ___

Lim - it - less, _ un - dy - ing love _ which shines a - round _ me like a mil - lion

D. S. al Coda

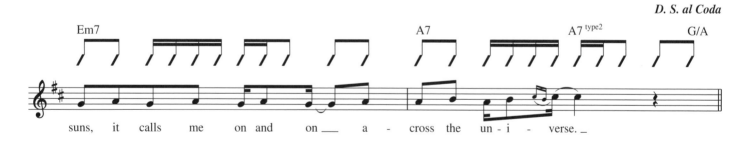

suns, it calls me on and on __ a - cross the un - i - verse. _

Coda

Play 6 Times And Fade

Jai ___ Gu - ru ___ De - va.

Against the Wind

Words and Music by Bob Seger

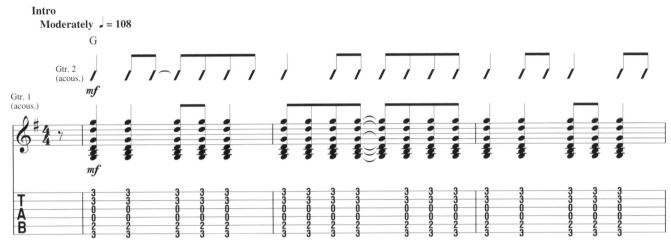

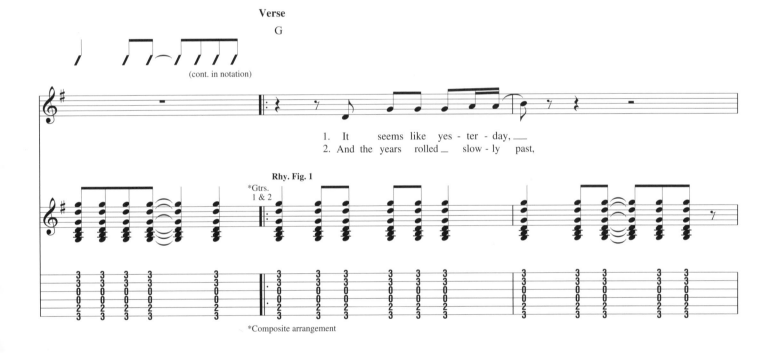

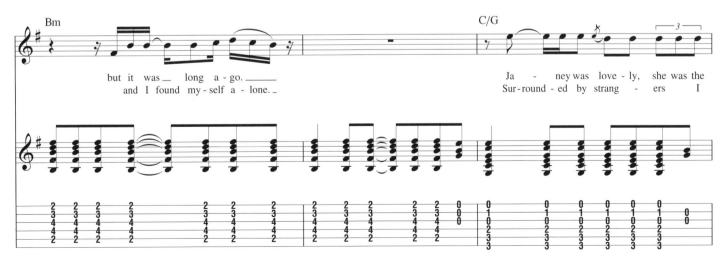

Pre-Chorus

3rd time, Gtr. 3: w/ Fill 1
3rd time, Gtr. 4 tacet

1. And I re - mem - ber _____ what she ___ said to me, _____ how she swore ___
2. Mov - ing eight ___ miles a min - ute ___ for months at a time, _____ break - ing all ___
   drift - er's days ___ are ___ past me now, I've got so ___

_____ that it nev - er would end.
_____ of the rules _____ that would bend.
_____ much more to think a - bout.

I re - mem-ber how she held ___ me, oh, ___
I be - gan to find my - self search -
Dead - lines and com -

_____ so tight. ___
- ing,
mit - ments,

Wish I did-n't know now what I did-n't know then. ___
search - ing for shel - ter a - gain ___ and a - gain. ___
what to leave in, _____ what to leave out. _

let ring - - - -|

Fill 1

Gtr. 3

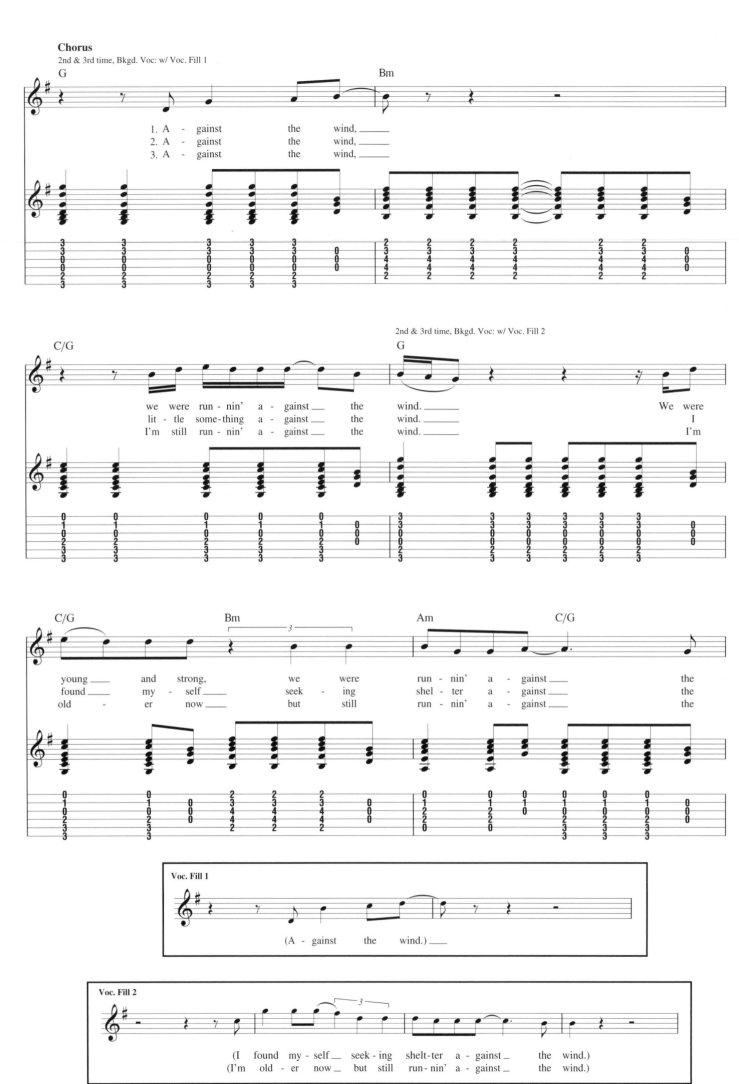

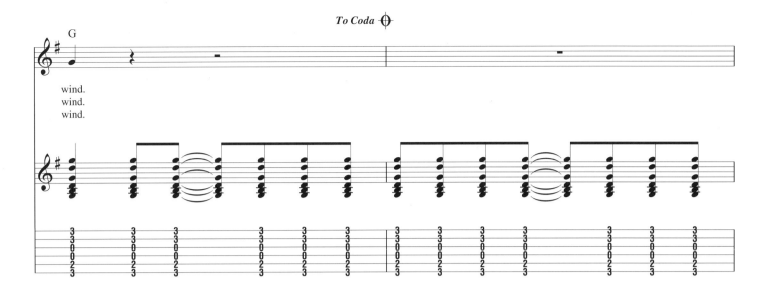

wind.
wind.
wind.

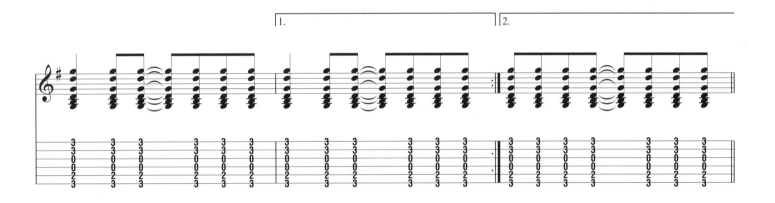

Piano Solo

Gtrs. 1 & 2: w/ Rhy. Fig. 1

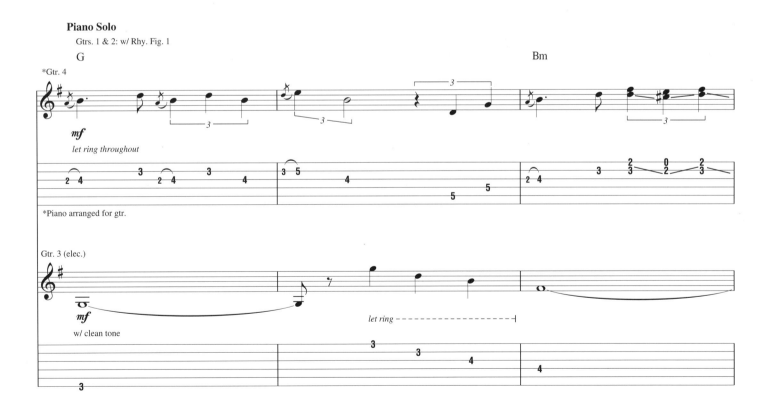

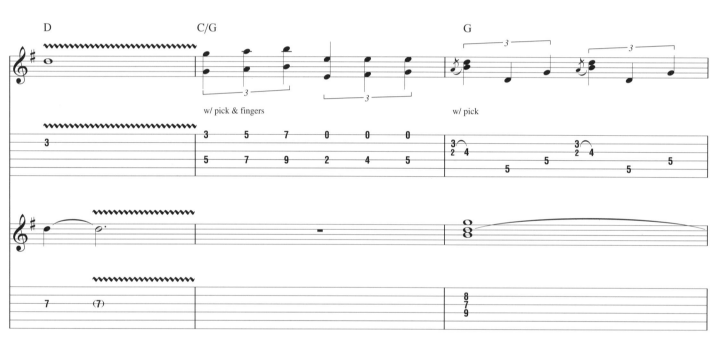

D.S. al Coda

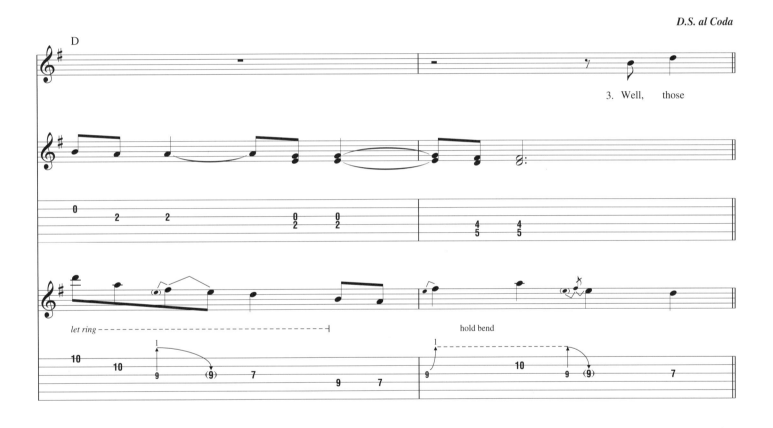

3. Well, those

Well, I'm old - er now _____ and still

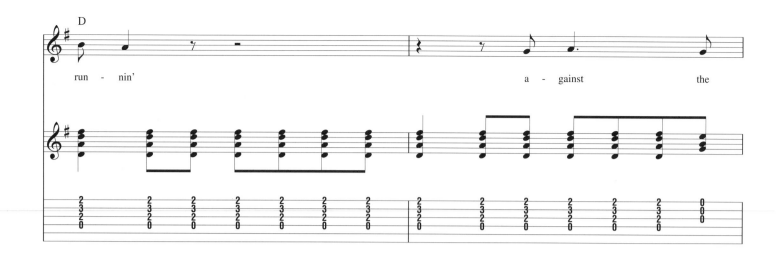

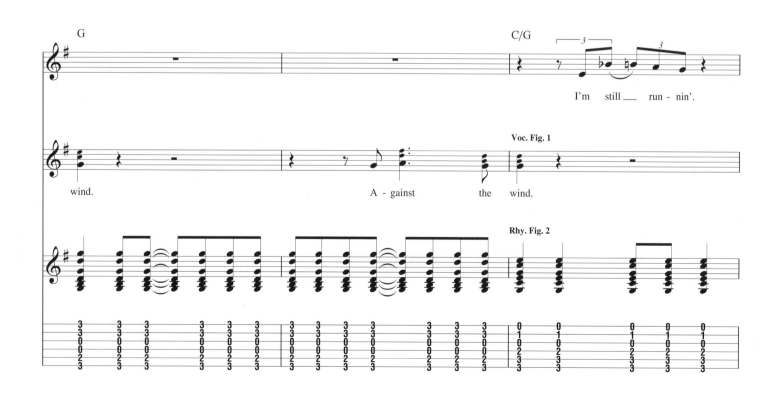

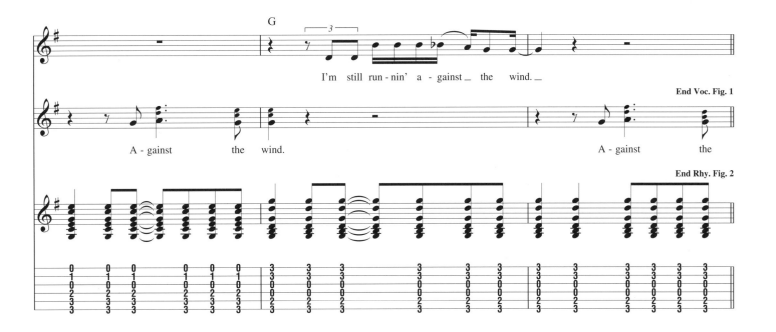

I'm still run - nin' a - gainst ___ the wind.

End Voc. Fig. 1

A - gainst the wind. A - gainst the

End Rhy. Fig. 2

5th time Fade out

Voc.: w/ Voc. Fig. 2 (till fade)
Gtrs. 1 & 2: w/ Rhy. Fig. 2 (till fade)

1. I'm still ___ run - nin'. ___
2.-5. *See additional lyrics*

I'm still run - nin' a - gainst ___ the wind. ___

___ Still run - nin'.

3rd time, Begin fade

Play 5 times

Run - nin' a - gainst ___ the wind, run - nin' a - gainst ___ the wind.

Additonal Lyrics

2. See the young man run.
 Watch the young man run.
 Watch the young man runnin'.
 They'll be runnin' against the wind.

3. Let the cowboys ride.
 Oo.
 Let the cowboys ride.
 They'll be ridin' against the wind.

4. Against the wind.
 Ridin' against the wind.

 Ride, ride, ride, ride, ride, ride, ride, ride, ride,

5. Ride, ride, ride.

Angie

Words and Music by Mick Jagger and Keith Richards

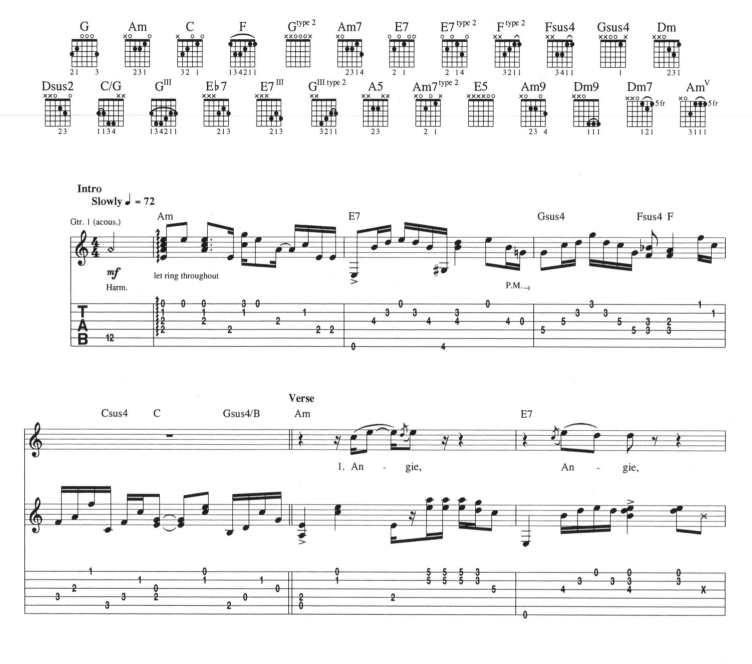

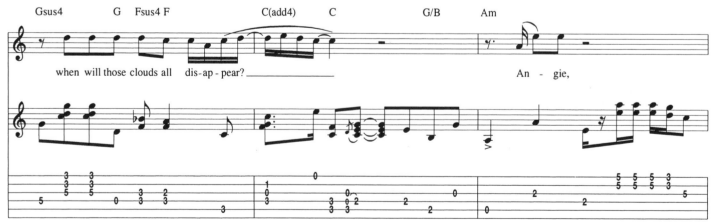

An - gie,   where will it lead us from here! _____

(Oh!)

Interlude

w/ pick and fingers

Gtr. 1

*Piano arr. for gtr.
**Violin arr. for gtr.
***Simulate bowing w/vol. pedal throughout.

Babe, I'm Gonna Leave You

Words and Music by Anne Bredon, Jimmy Page and Robert Plant

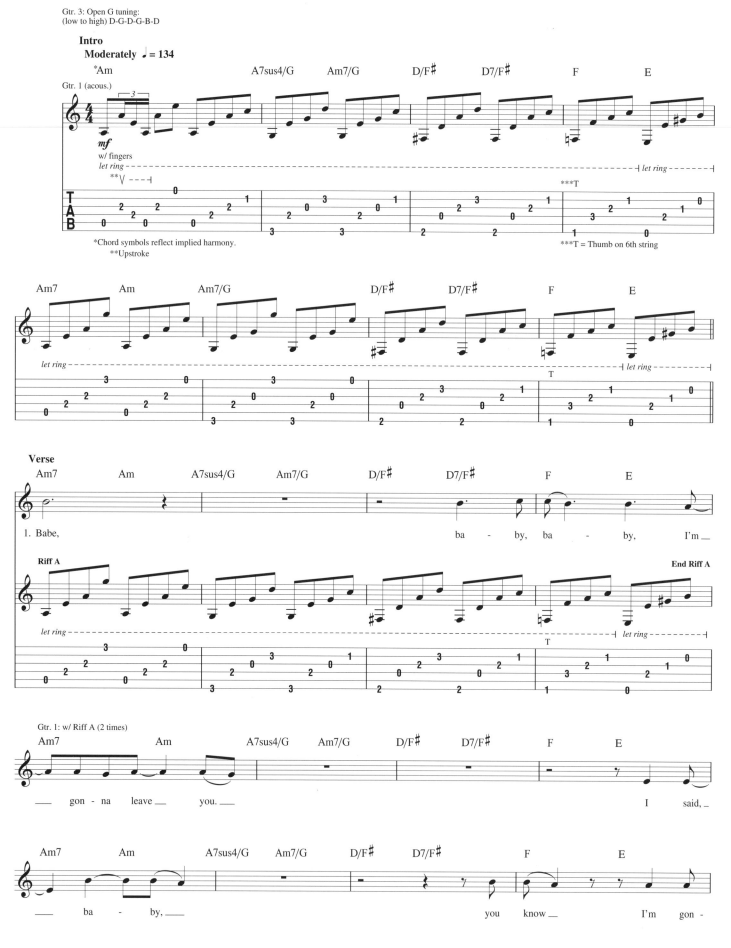

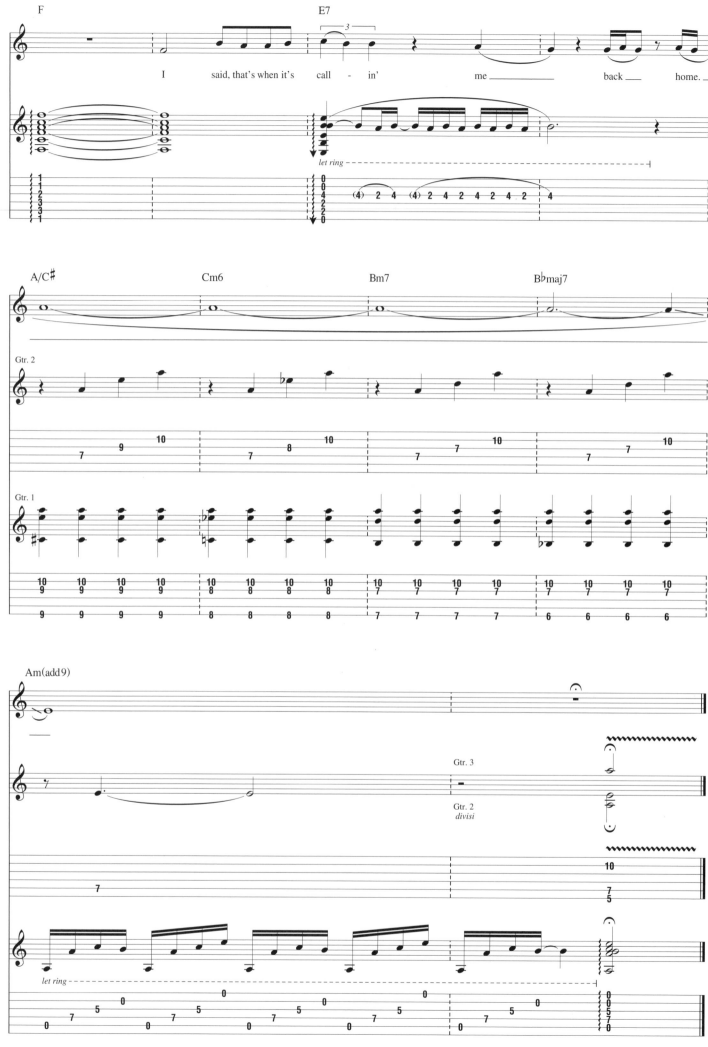

Behind Blue Eyes

Words and Music by Pete Townshend

fat - ed ___ to tell - ing on - ly lies. But my

Chorus

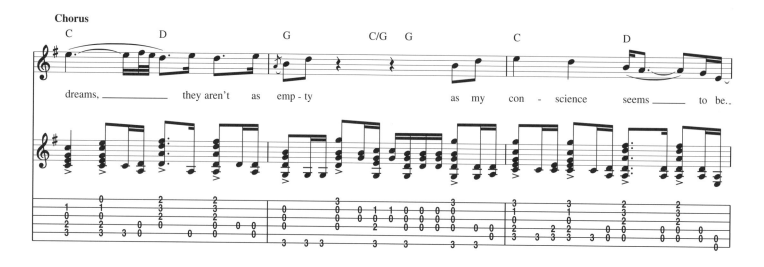

dreams, ___ they aren't as emp - ty as my con - science seems ___ to be..

___ I have hours ___ on - ly lone - ly. ___ My love is ven -

- geance that's nev - er free. 2. N -

* vib w/ neck

* Vibrato achieved by applying force with right hand on gtr. body & left hand on neck.

Outro
Half-Time ♩ = 60

Gtr. 2 tacet

N - no one knows what it's like to be the

bad   man, _   to be the sad   man _   be-hind _ blue eyes. _

poco rit.

Breaking the Girl

Words and Music by Anthony Kiedis, Flea, John Frusciante and Chad Smith

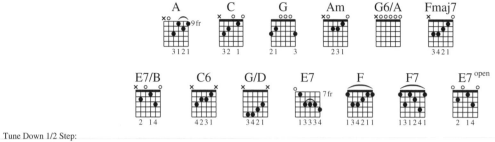

Tune Down 1/2 Step:

① = E♭ ④ = D♭
② = B♭ ⑤ = A♭
③ = G♭ ⑥ = E♭

Intro

Moderately ♩. = 60

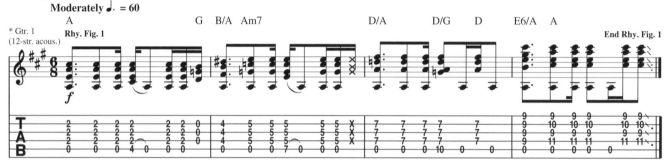

* Gtr. 1 (12-str. acous.)

* Two gtrs. arr. for one.

Verse

Gtr. 1: w/ Rhy. Fig. 1, 4 times, simile

1. I _____ am a man _____ cut from ___ the know. _____ Rare - ly do friends _____
2. Raised ___ by my dad, _____ girl of ____ the day. He ___ was my man, _____

come and ___ then go. _____ She _____ was a girl _____ soft _____ but es - tranged. _____
that was ___ the way. _____ She _____ was the girl _____ left _____ a - lone. _____

We were the two _____ our lives _____ re - ar - ranged. _____
Feel - ing no need _____ to make _____ me her home. _____

Pre-Chorus

Feel-ing so good _____ that day. _____ A feel - ing of
I don't know what, _____ when or why. _____ The twi - light of

Crazy on You

Words and Music by Ann Wilson, Nancy Wilson and Roger Fisher

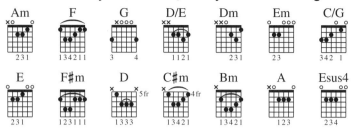

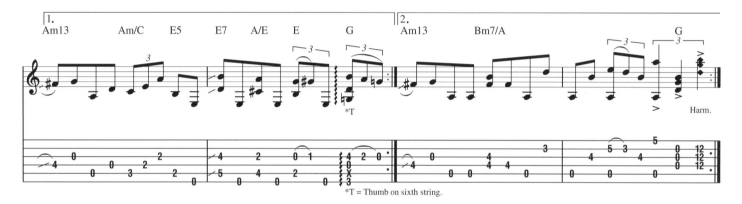

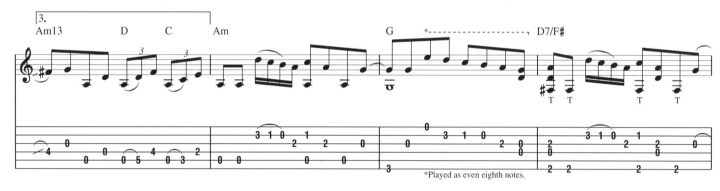

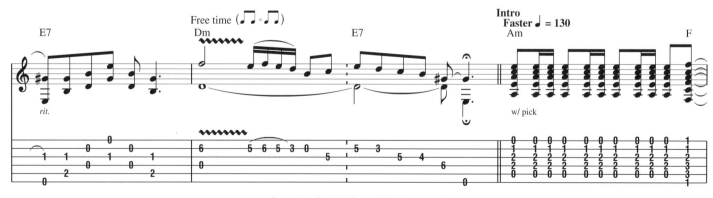

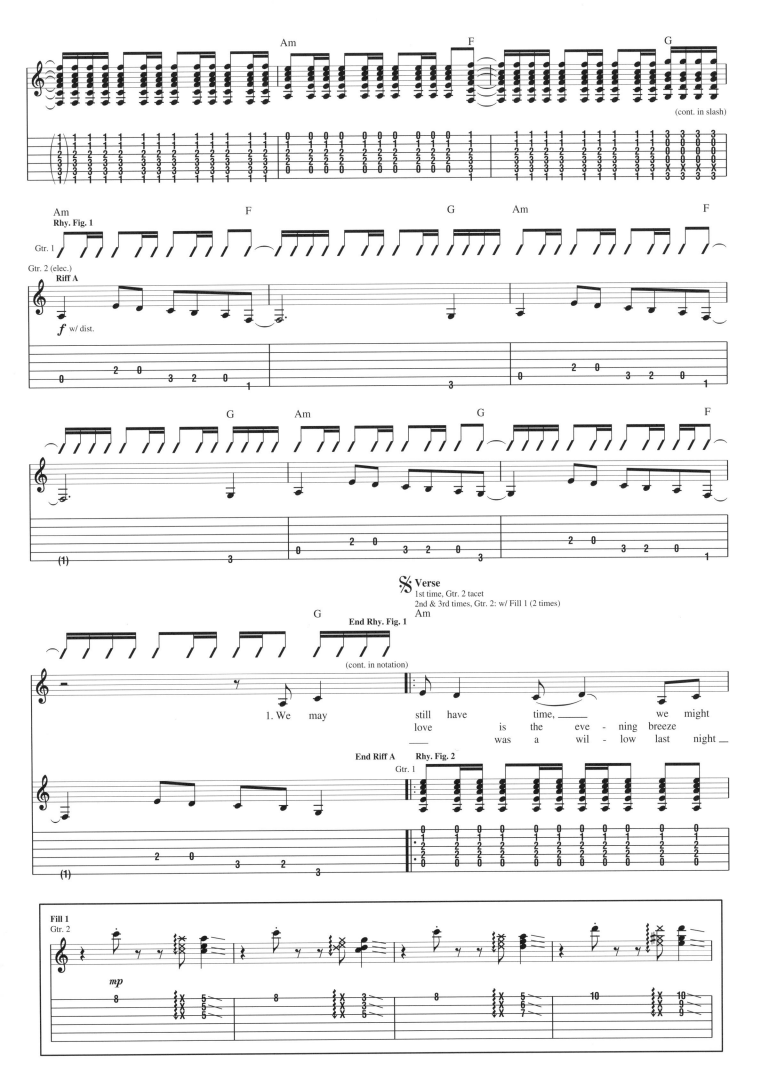

cry - ing in pain, what - cha gon-na do ____ when ev - 'ry - bod - y's in - sane? ____

Oo.

So a-fraid of won - ders, so a - fraid of you, what-cha gon - na do? ____

Oo. ____ Oo.

Riff B

Gtr. 2 tacet

Gtr. 3

⊕ Coda

Chorus
Gtr. 1: w/ Rhy. Fig. 1 (1st 6 meas.)
Gtr. 2: w/ Riff A (1st 6 meas.)

sweet flow-ing love. _____ Yeah. _____ cra - zy, on
Cra - zy, _____

Gtr. 1: w/ Rhy. Fill 1 (1st meas.)
Gtr. 2: w/ Fill 2 (1st meas.)

you. Let me go cra - zy, cra - zy on you, _____ oo. _____ Cra -

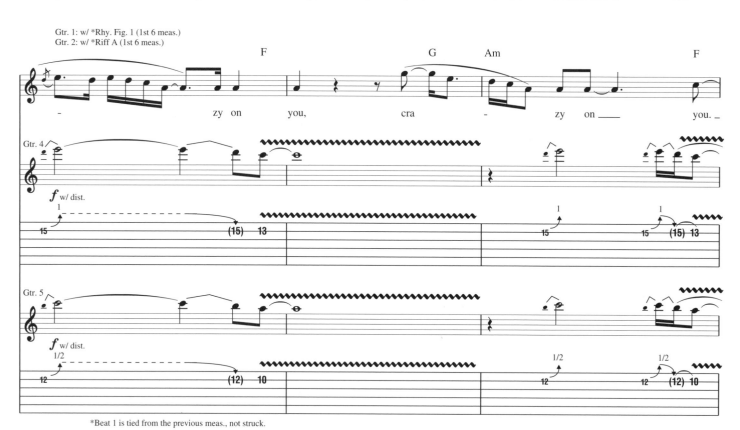

Gtr. 1: w/ *Rhy. Fig. 1 (1st 6 meas.)
Gtr. 2: w/ *Riff A (1st 6 meas.)

- zy on you, cra - zy on _____ you.

*Beat 1 is tied from the previous meas., not struck.

Gtr. 1: w/ Rhy. Fill 1 (1st meas.)
Gtr. 2: w/ Fill 2 (1st meas.)

_____ Let me go cra - zy, cra - zy on you, _____ yeah. _____

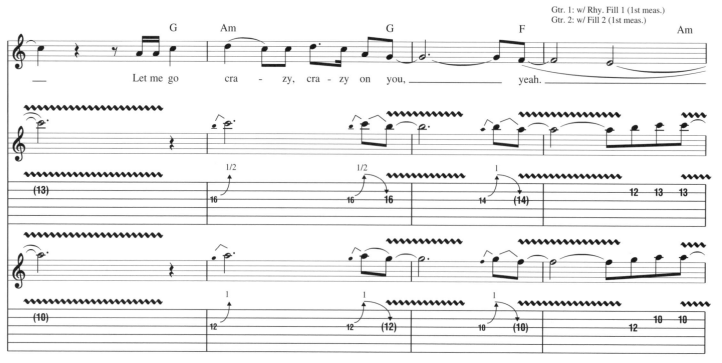

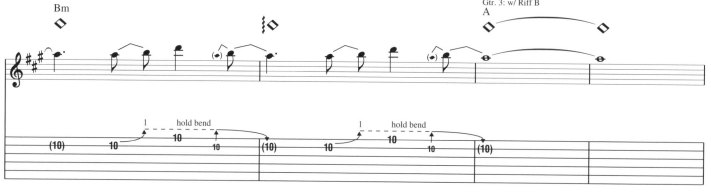

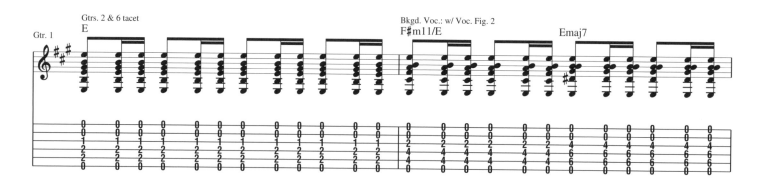

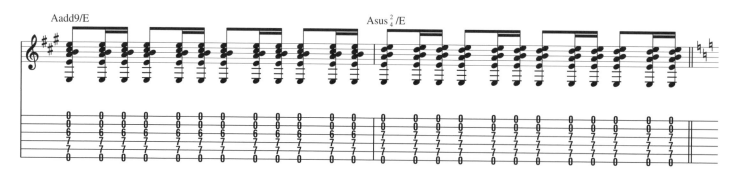

Outro-Chorus

Gtr. 1: w/ Rhy. Fig. 1 (1st 6 meas.)
Gtr. 2: w/ Riff A (1st 6 meas.)

Am   F   G   Am   F   G

Cra - zy on you,   cra - zy on ___ you. ___   Let me go

Gtr. 1: w/ *Rhy. Fill 1
Gtr. 2: w/ *Fill 2

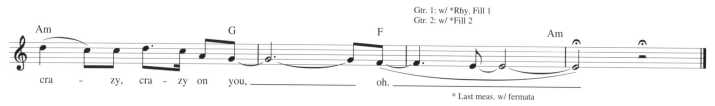

Am   G   F   Am

cra - zy, cra-zy on you, _____ oh. _____

* Last meas. w/ fermata

Daughter

Words and Music by Stone Gossard, Jeffrey Ament, Eddie Vedder, Michael McCready and David Abbruzzese

*See top of first page of song for chord diagrams pertaining to rhythm slashes.

Chorus

Gtr. 1: w/ Rhy. Fig. 1 (2 times)
Gtr. 2: w/ Rhy. Fig. 2 (2 times)
Gtr. 4 tacet

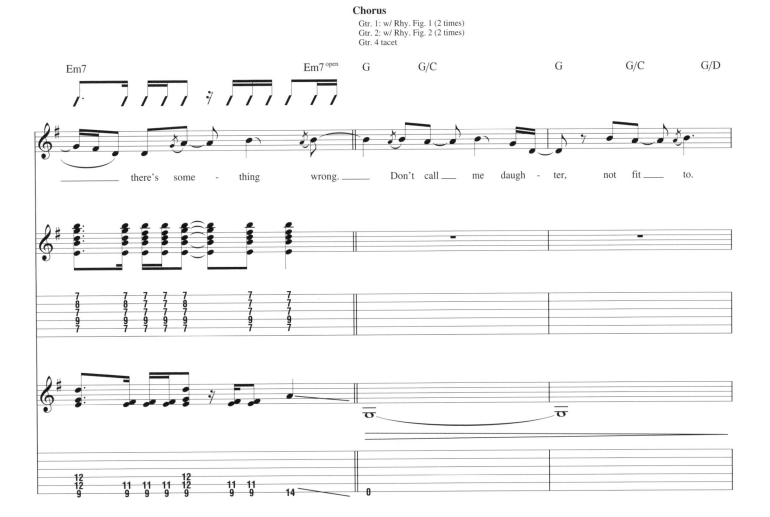

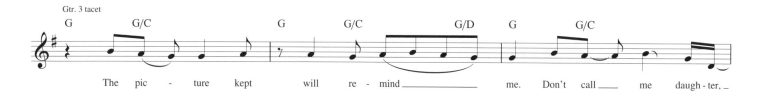

The pic - ture kept will re - mind _____ me. Don't call ____ me daugh - ter, __

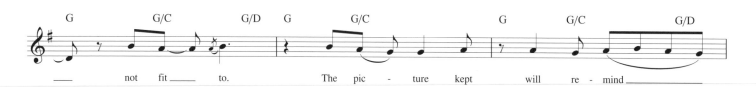

____ not fit ____ to. The pic - ture kept will re - mind _____

Interlude

Gtr. 1: w/ Rhy. Fill 1
Gtr. 2: w/ Rhy. Fill 2
Gtr. 3: w/ Fill 1

Gtrs. 2 & 4: w/ Rhy. Fig. 3
Gtr. 3: w/ Rhy. Fig. 4

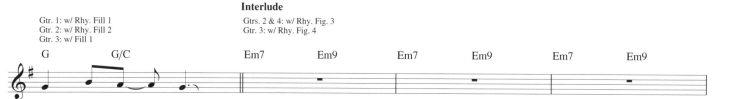

me. Don't call ____ me...

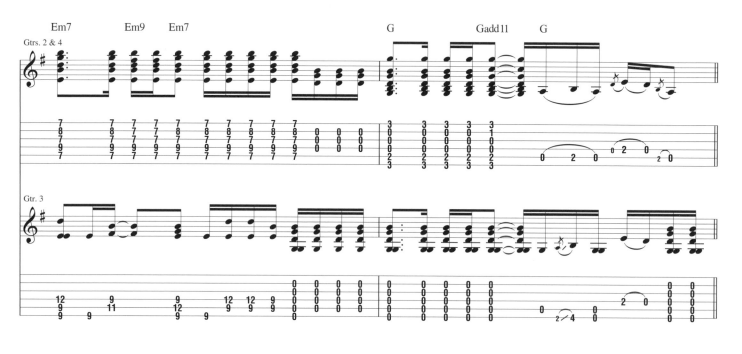

Bridge

Gtr. 4: w/ Rhy. Fig. 3B

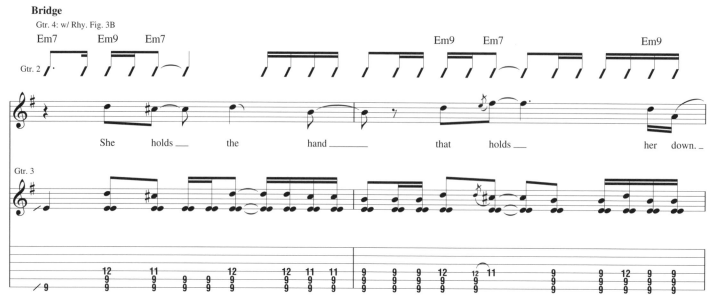

She holds ____ the hand _____ that holds ____ her down. __

Gtr. 4: w/ Rhy. Fig. 3B (last meas.)

Em7   Em9   Em7   Em7 open

ff
w/ dist.

(cont. in notation)

She will ___ rise ___ a - bove. ___

(cont. in slashes)

Guitar Solo

Gtr. 1: w/ Rhy. Fig. 1 (2 times)

G

Gtr. 3

Oo.

Gtr. 2

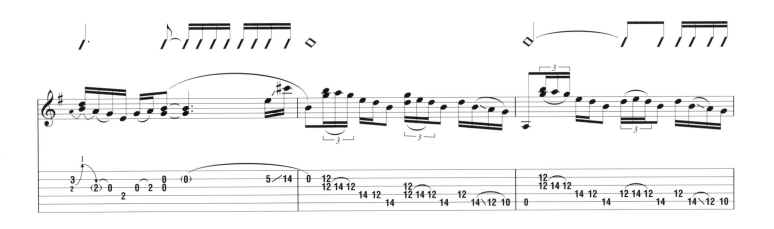

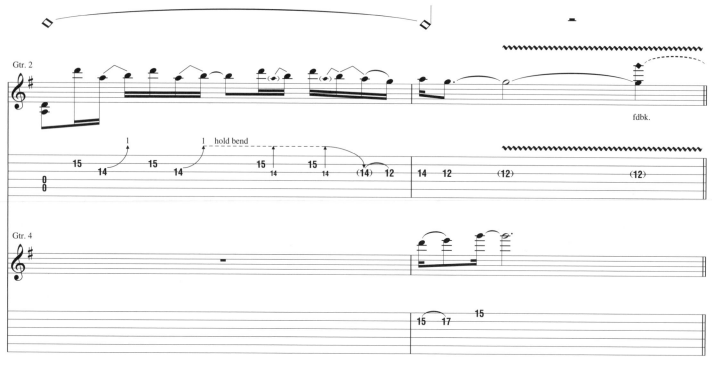

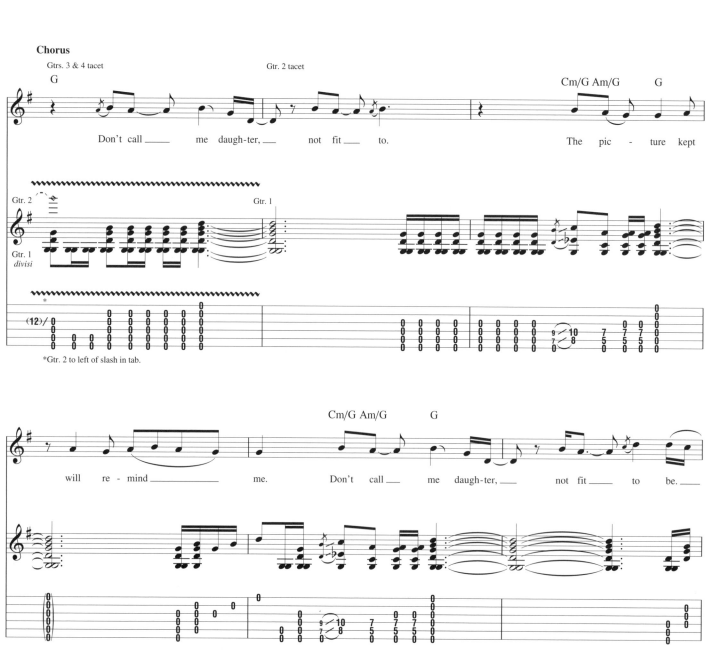

Interlude

Disarm

Words and Music by Billy Corgan

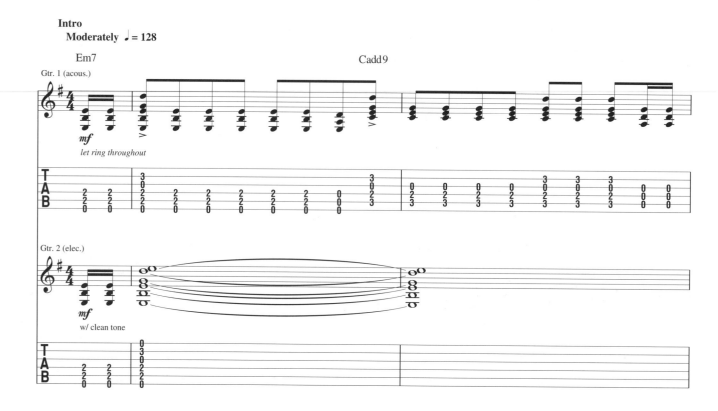

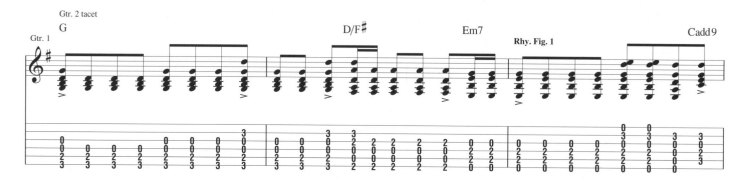

Dust in the Wind

Words and Music by Kerry Livgren

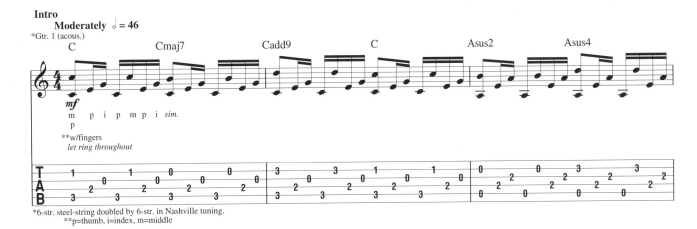

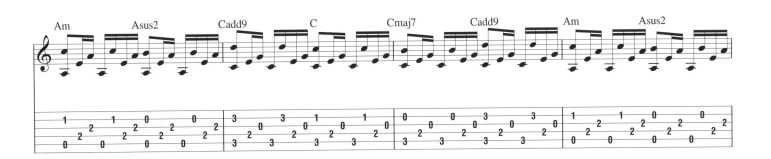

Every Rose Has Its Thorn

Words and Music by Bobby Dall, Brett Michaels, Bruce Johannesson and Rikki Rockett

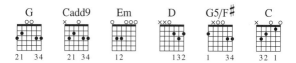

Tune down 1/2 step:
(low to high) E♭-A♭-D♭-G♭-B♭-E♭

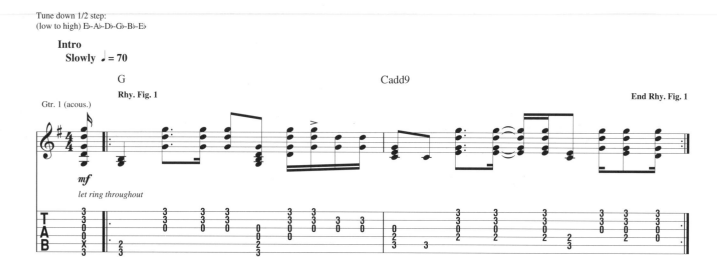

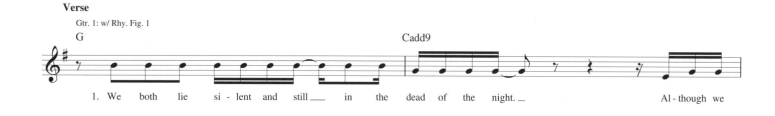

1. We both lie si-lent and still ___ in the dead of the night. ___ Al-though we

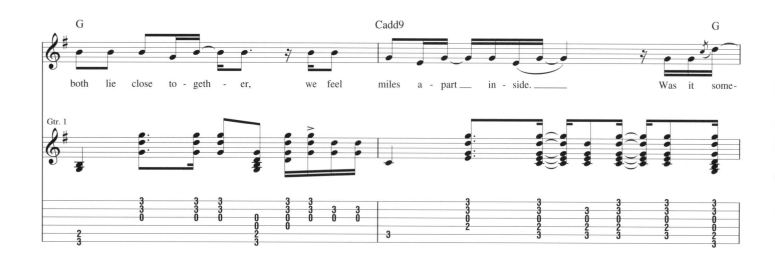

both lie close to-geth-er, we feel miles a-part ___ in-side. ___ Was it some-

-thin' I said or some-thin' I did? Did my words __ not come out right? __ Though I tried __

__ not to hurt __ you, __ though I tried. __ But I guess __ that's why __ they say

Chorus

Gtr. 1: w/ Rhy. Fig. 1 (1 1/2 times)

ev - 'ry rose __ has its thorn, __ just like ev - 'ry night __ has its dawn. __

Just like ev - 'ry cow-boy sings a sad, __ sad __ song, __

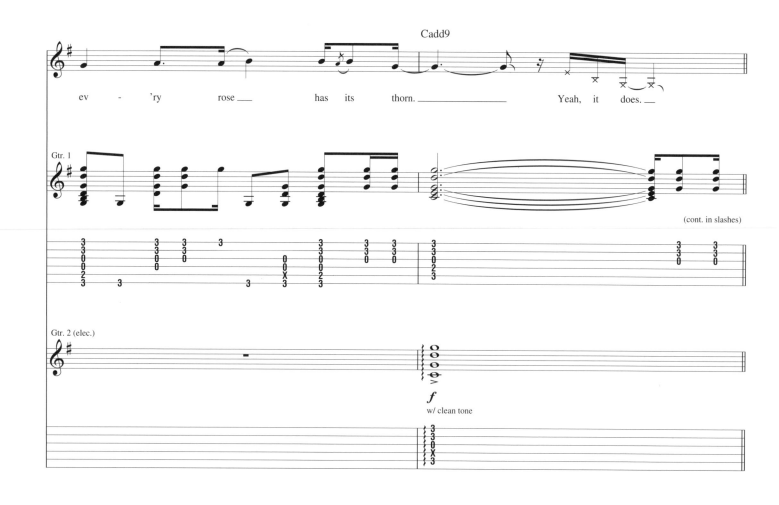

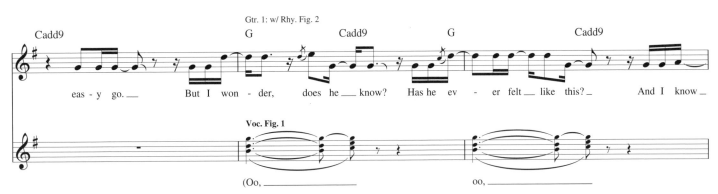

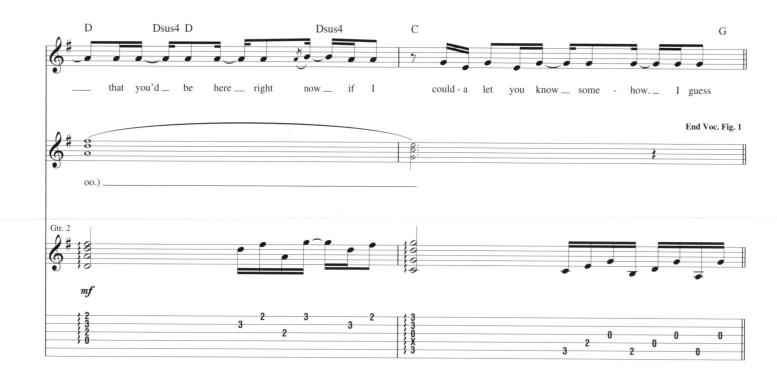

that you'd be here right now if I could-a let you know some-how. I guess

End Voc. Fig. 1

oo.)

Gtr. 2

mf

Chorus

Gtr. 1: w/ Rhy. Fig. 1 (2 times)

ev - 'ry rose has its thorn, just like ev-

Riff A

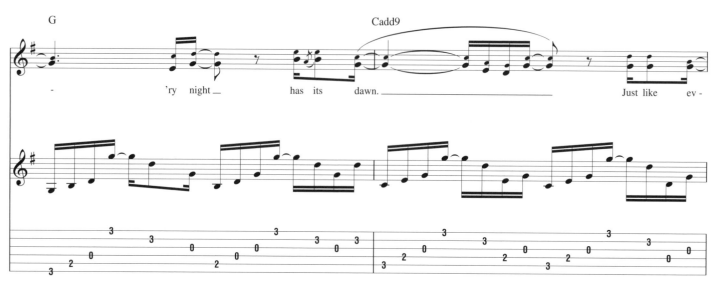

- 'ry night has its dawn. Just like ev-

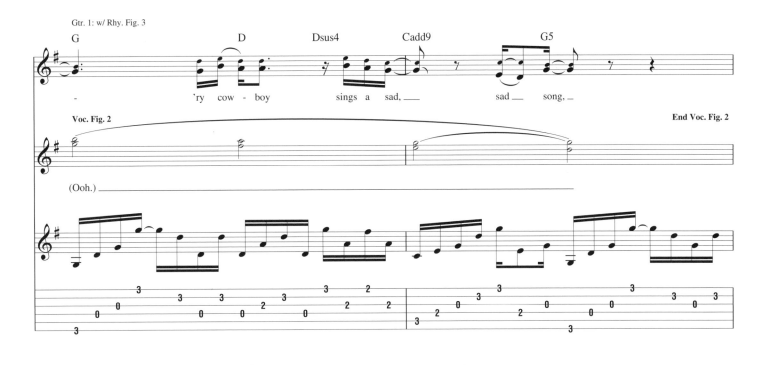

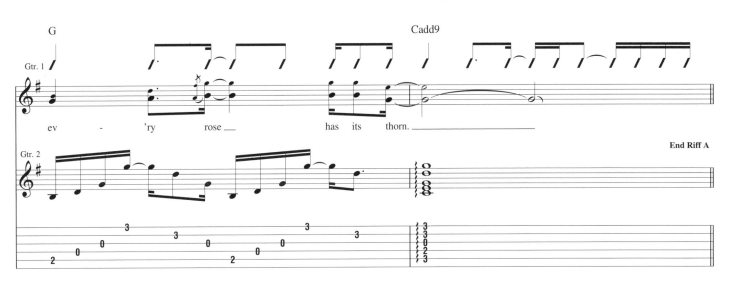

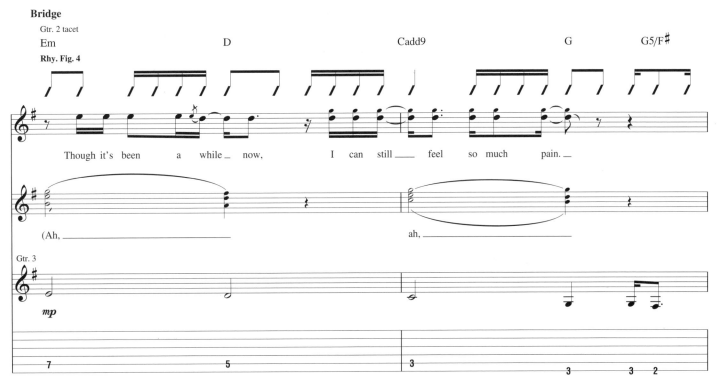

Chorus

Gtr. 1: w/ Rhy. Fig. 1 (2 times)
Gtr. 2: w/ Riff A

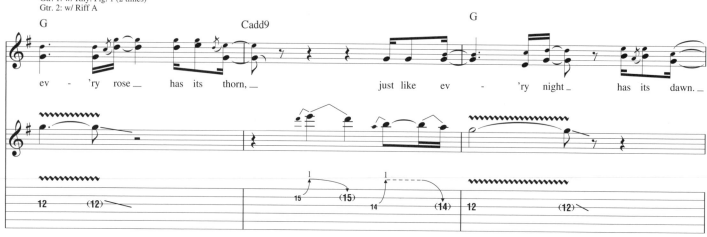

ev - 'ry rose __ has its thorn, __ just like ev - 'ry night __ has its dawn. __

Bkgd. Voc.: w/ Voc. Fig. 2
Gtr. 1: w/ Rhy. Fig. 3

Just like ev - 'ry cow - boy sings a sad, __ sad __ song, __

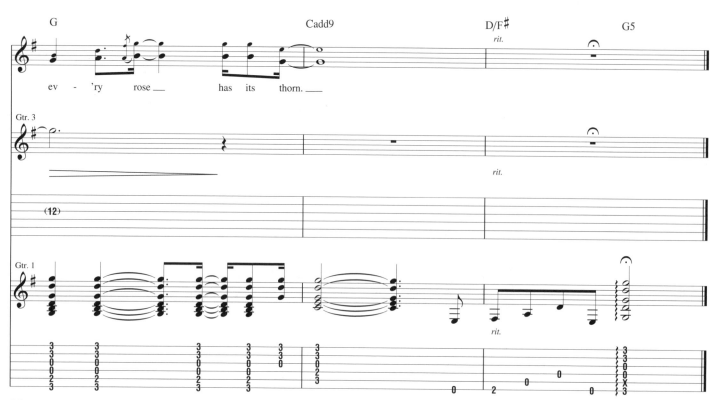

ev - 'ry rose __ has its thorn. __

Foolin'

Words and Music by Joe Elliott, Steve Clark, Peter Willis, Richard Savage, Richard Allen and Robert Lange

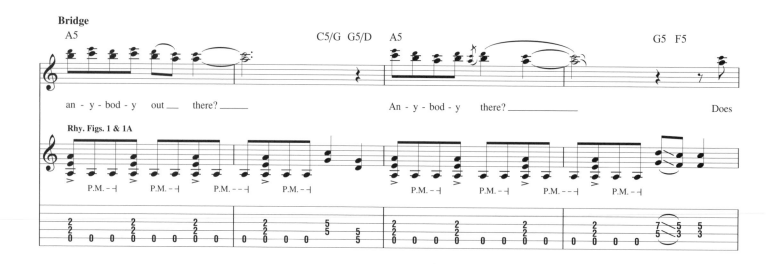

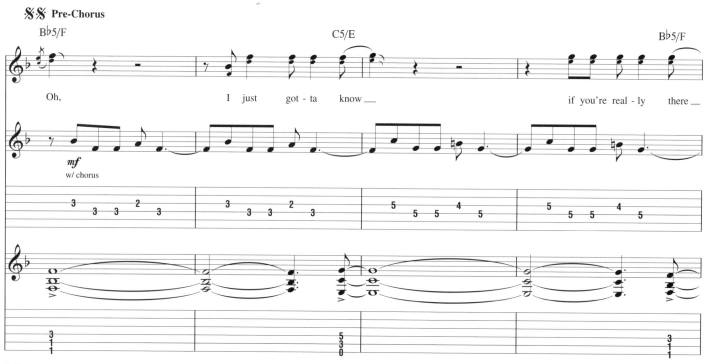

Interlude

*See top of first page of song for chord diagrams pertaining to rhythm slashes.

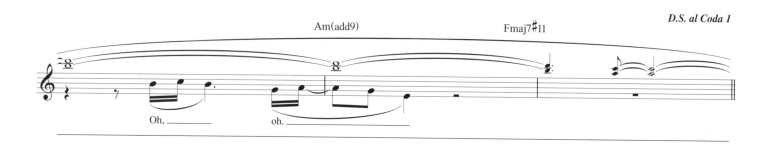

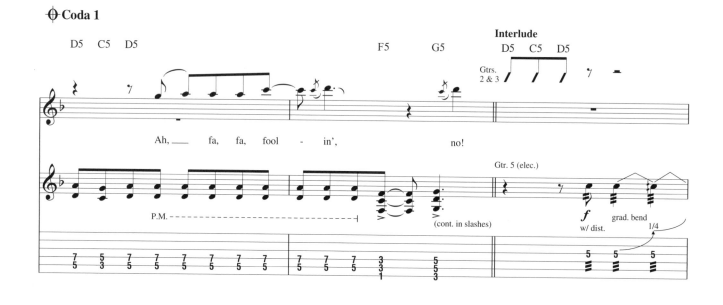

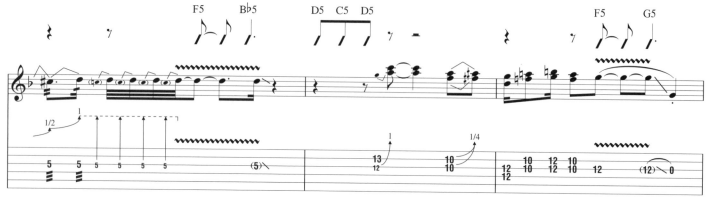

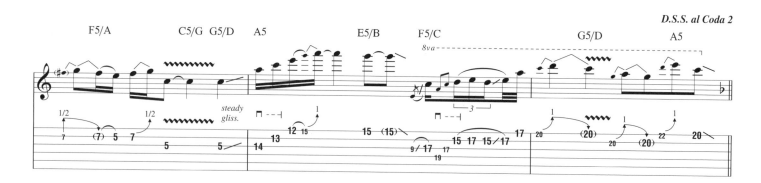

⊕ Coda 2

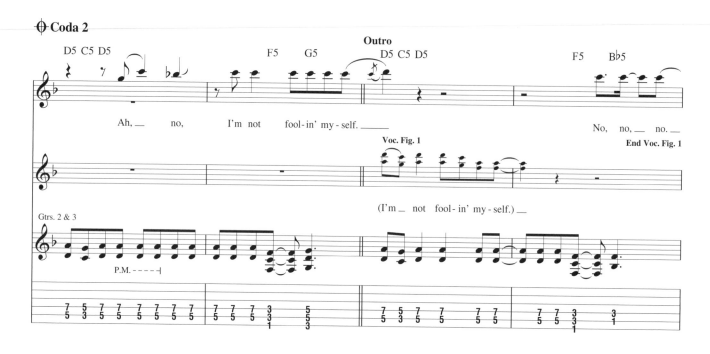

Free Fallin'

Words and Music by Tom Petty and Jeff Lynne

Capo I

Intro

Moderately Slow ♩ = 84

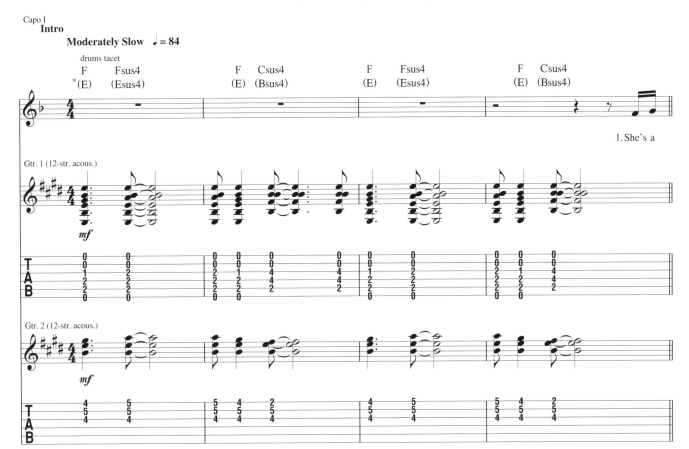

1. She's a

*Symbols in parentheses represent chord names respective to capoed guitar.
Symbols above reflect actual sounding chord. Capoed fret is "0" in TAB.

Verse

Gtrs. 1 & 2: w/ Rhy. Figs. 1 & 1A, 4 times, simile

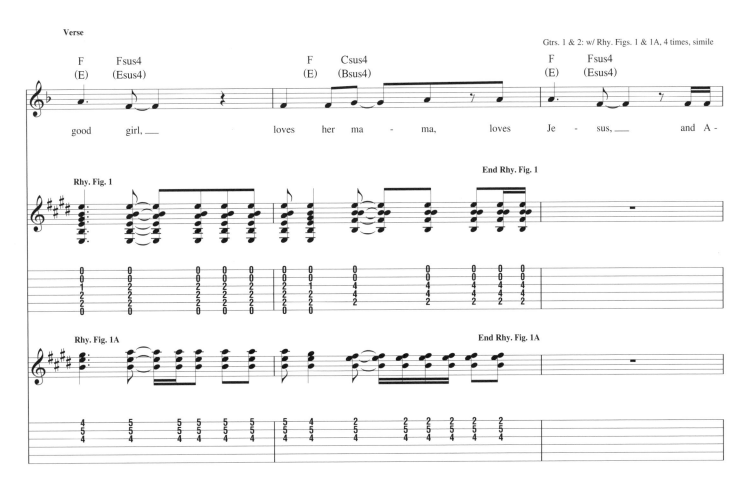

good girl, ___ loves her ma - ma, loves Je - sus, ___ and A -

Have You Ever Seen the Rain?

Words and Music by John Fogerty

Intro
Moderately ♩ = 116

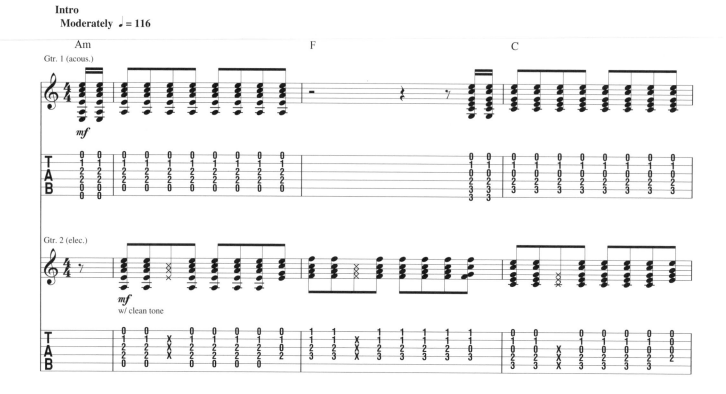

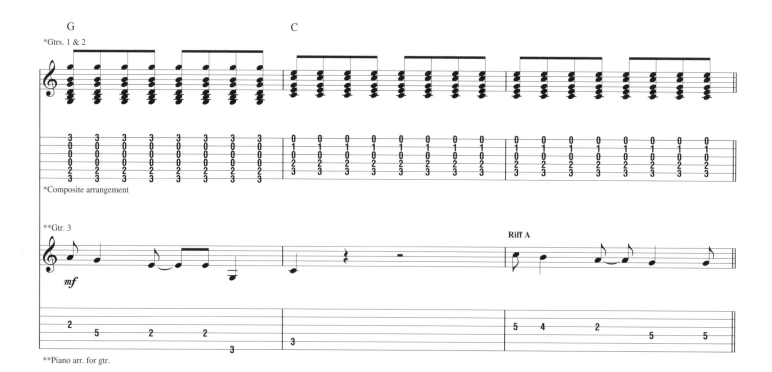

*Composite arrangement

**Piano arr. for gtr.

Verse

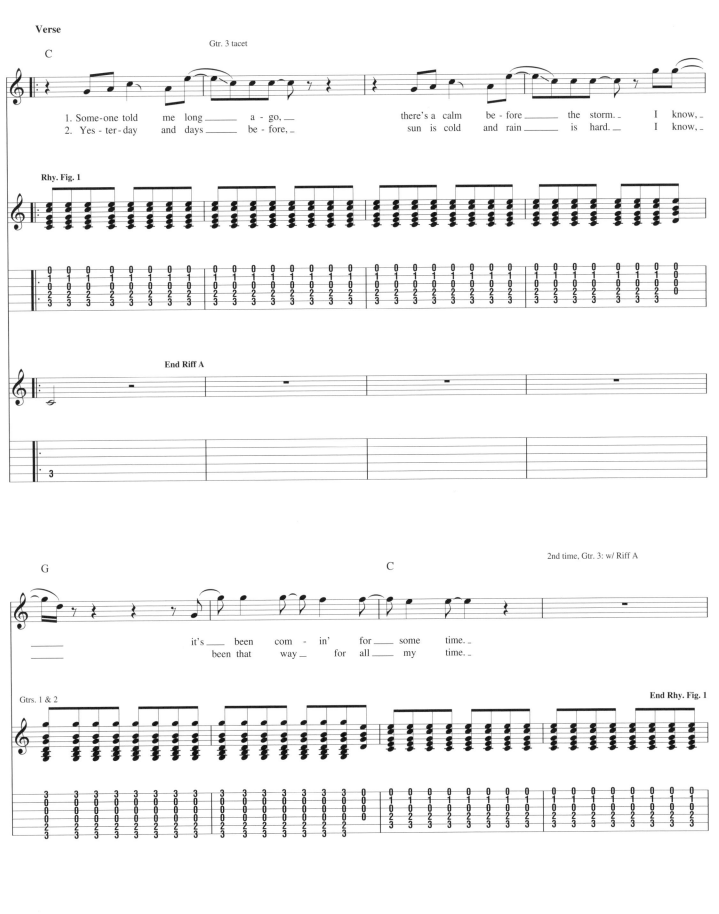

1. Some-one told me long ____ a - go, ____ there's a calm be - fore ____ the storm. ___ I know, ___
2. Yes - ter - day and days ____ be - fore, ___ sun is cold and rain ____ is hard. ___ I know, ___

2nd time, Gtr. 3: w/ Riff A

it's ___ been com - in' for ___ some time. ____
been that way ___ for all ___ my time. ___

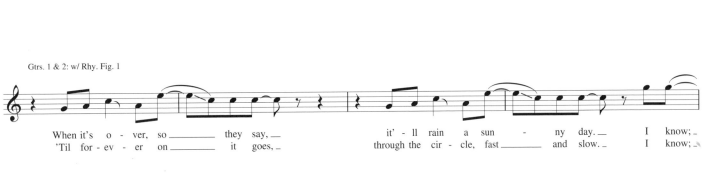

When it's o - ver, so ____ they say, ___ it' - ll rain a sun - ny day. ___ I know; ___
'Til for - ev - er on ____ it goes, ___ through the cir - cle, fast ____ and slow. ___ I know; ___

shin - in' down ___ like wa - ter.
it ___ can't stop, ___ I won - der.

Chorus

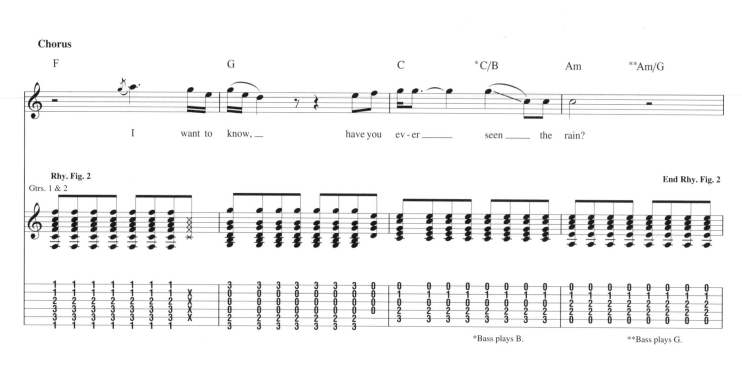

I want to know, ___ have you ev - er ___ seen ___ the rain?

Rhy. Fig. 2
Gtrs. 1 & 2
End Rhy. Fig. 2

*Bass plays B.   **Bass plays G.

Gtrs. 1 & 2: w/ Rhy. Fig. 2

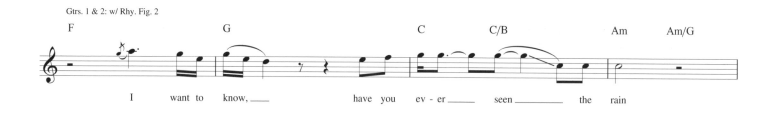

I want to know, ___ have you ev - er ___ seen ___ the rain

1.

Gtr. 3: w/ Riff A

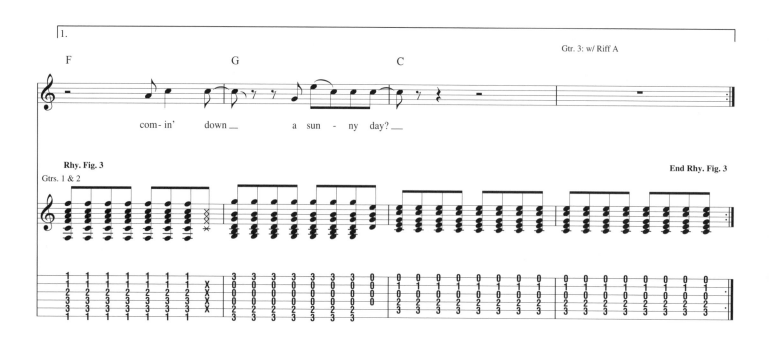

com - in' down ___ a sun - ny day? ___

Rhy. Fig. 3
Gtrs. 1 & 2
End Rhy. Fig. 3

Heaven Beside You

Lyrics by Jerry Cantrell
Music by Jerry Cantrell and Mike Inez

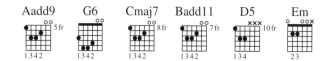

Aadd9 G6 Cmaj7 Badd11 D5 Em

Tune Down 1/2 Step:
① = Eb   ④ = Db
② = Bb   ⑤ = Ab
③ = Gb   ⑥ = Eb

Intro
Moderately ♩ = 110

Verse

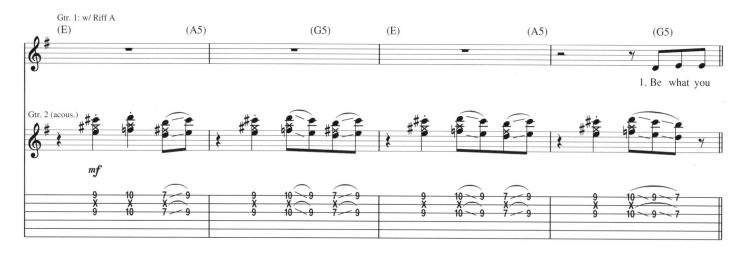

wan-na be.
wan-na do.

See what you came to see.
Go out and seek your truth.

Been what you
When I'm

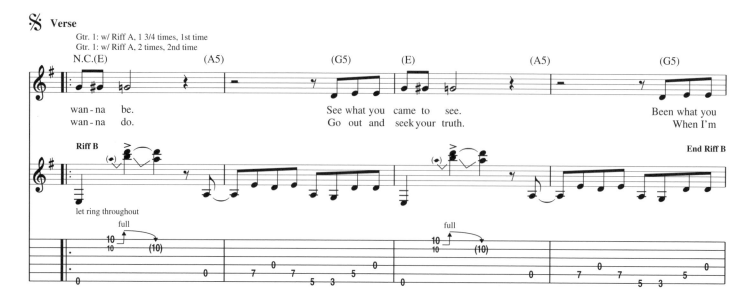

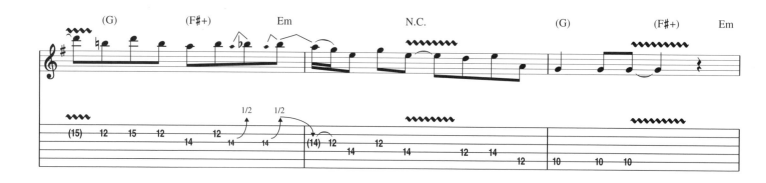

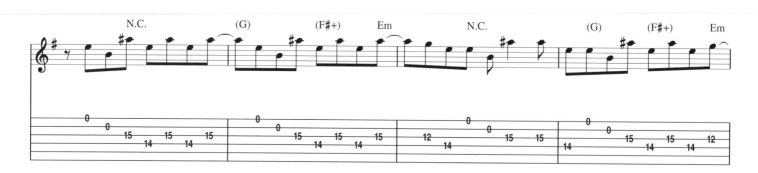

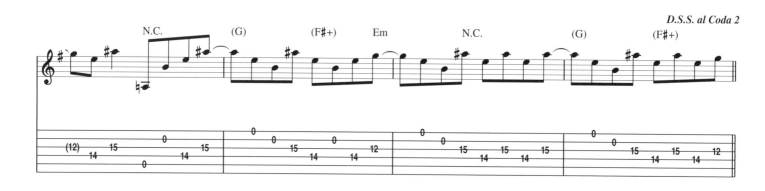

D.S.S. al Coda 2

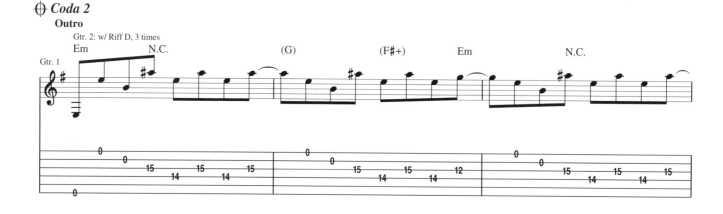

⊕ *Coda 2*
Outro

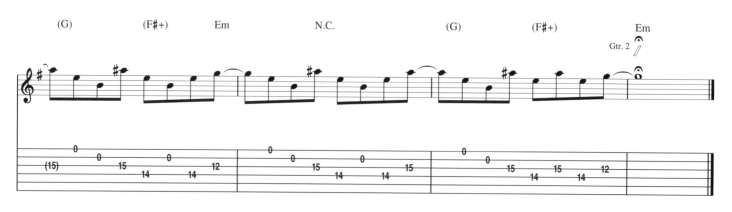

I'd Love to Change the World

Words and Music by Alvin Lee

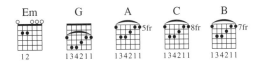

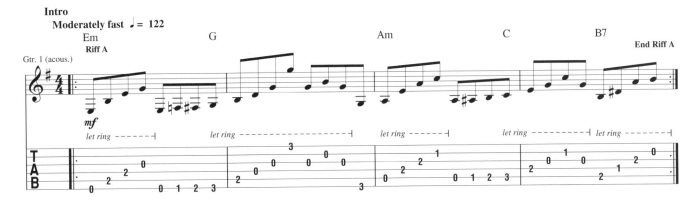

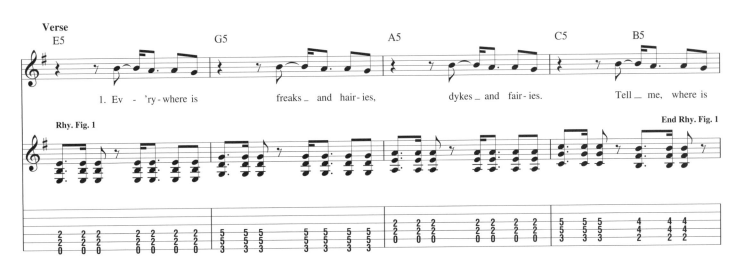

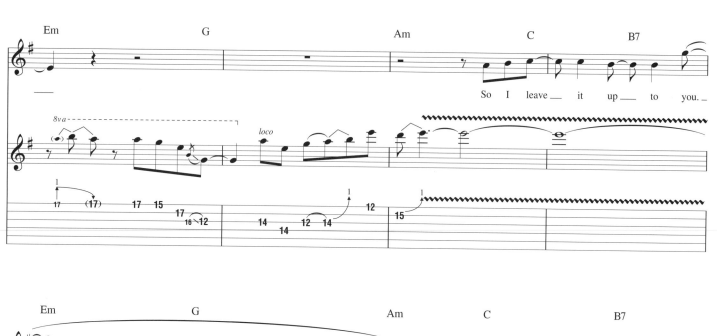

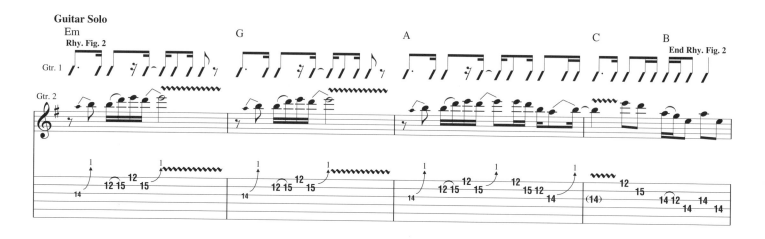

Guitar Solo
Gtr. 1: w/ Riff A (2 times)

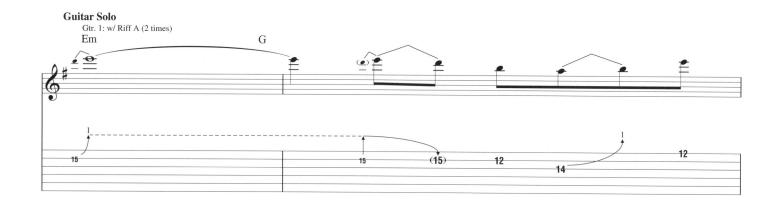

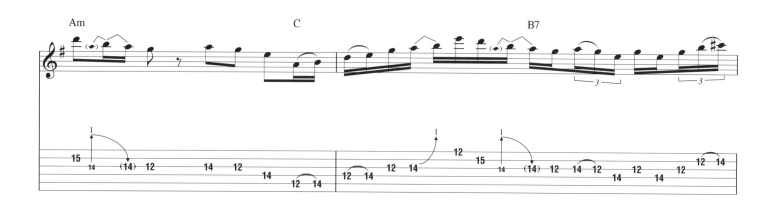

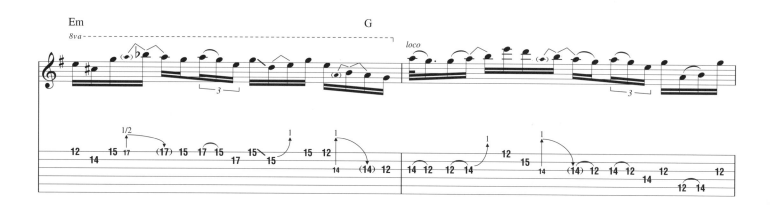

Iris

from the Motion Picture CITY OF ANGELS

Words and Music by John Rzeznik

Gtr. 1 Tuning:
(low to high) D-D-D-D-D-B

Intro

Moderately Slow ♩. = 51

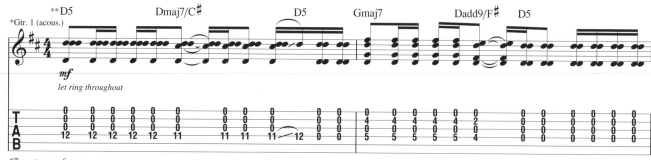

*Two gtrs. arr. for one.
**Chord symbols reflect implied harmony.

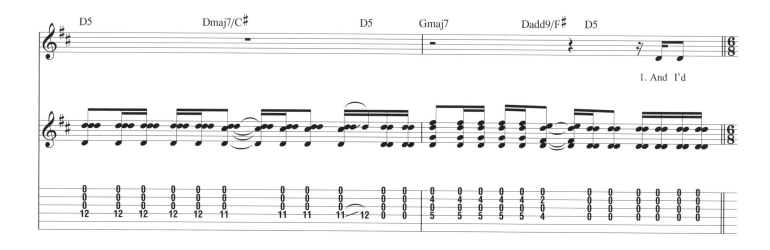

1. And I'd

Verse

give up for-ev-er to touch __ you 'cause I know __ that you feel __ me some - how. You're the clos-

Riff A   **End Riff A**

Gtr. 1: w/ Riff A, 3 times, simile

-est to heav - en that I'll __ ev - er be, __ and I don't __ wan-na go __ home right now. And all __

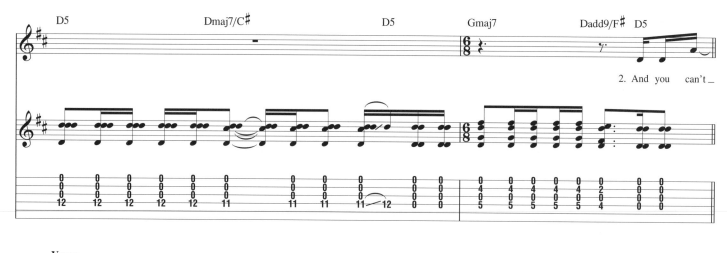

2. And you can't _

Verse

Gtr. 1: w/ Riff A, 2 times, simile

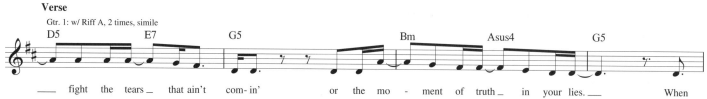

_ fight the tears _ that ain't com-in' or the mo - ment of truth _ in your lies. _ When

D.S. al Coda 1

ev - 'ry - thing feels like the mov - ies, yeah, you bleed _ just to know _ you're a - live. _ And I

Coda 1

Interlude

Gtr. 1

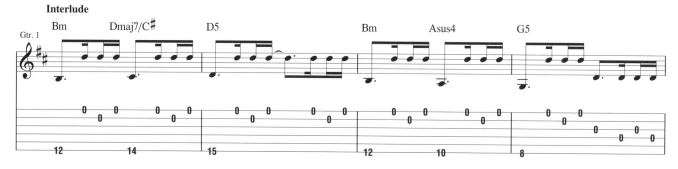

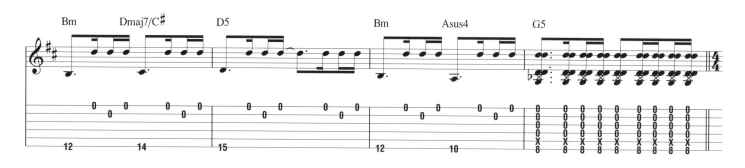

Play 5 times

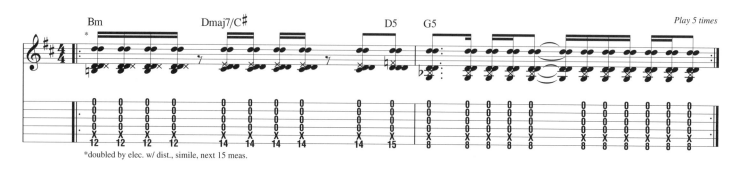

*doubled by elec. w/ dist., simile, next 15 meas.

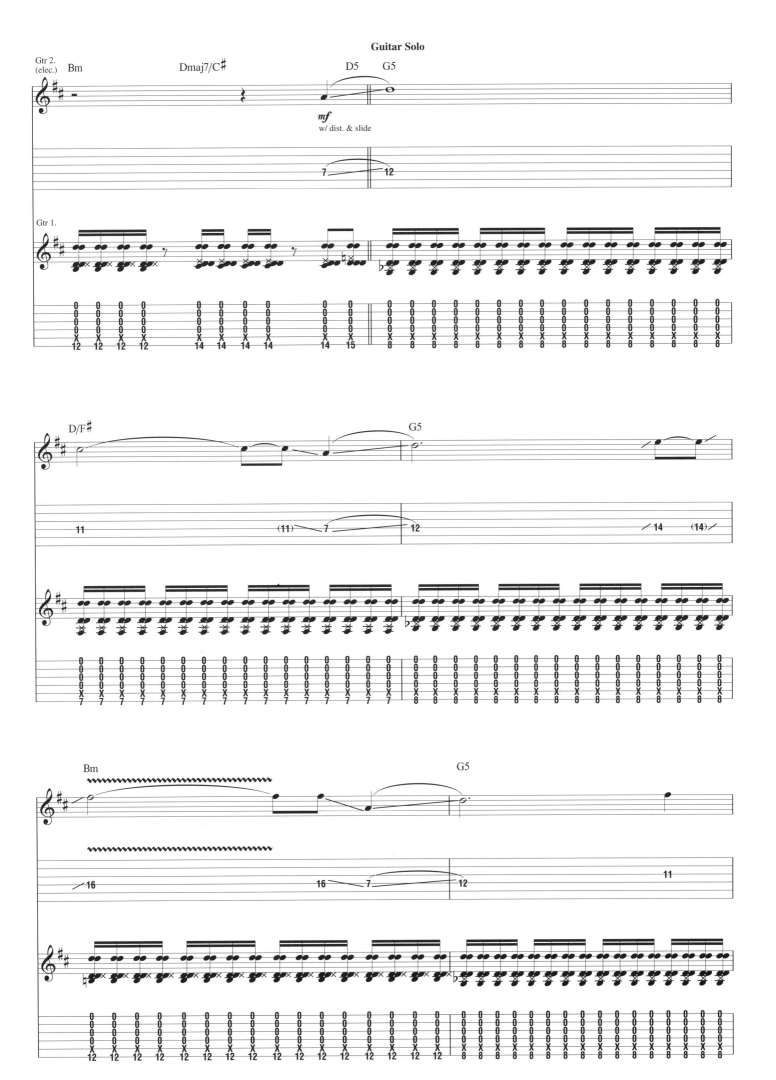

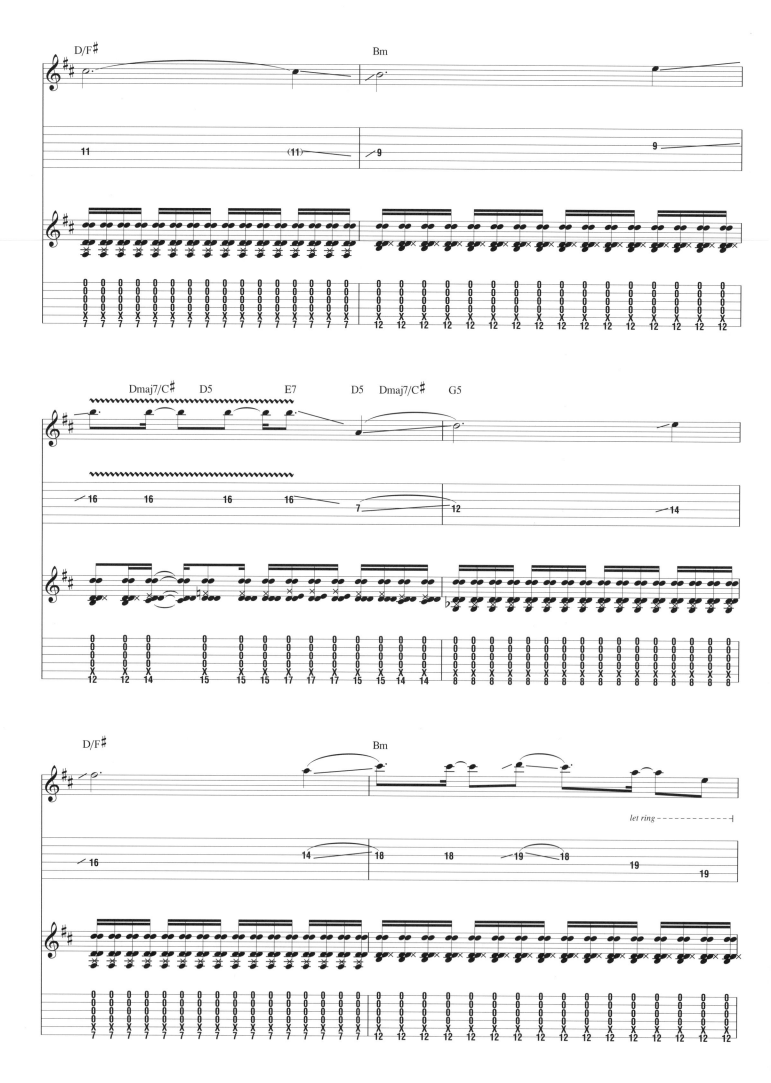

Interlude

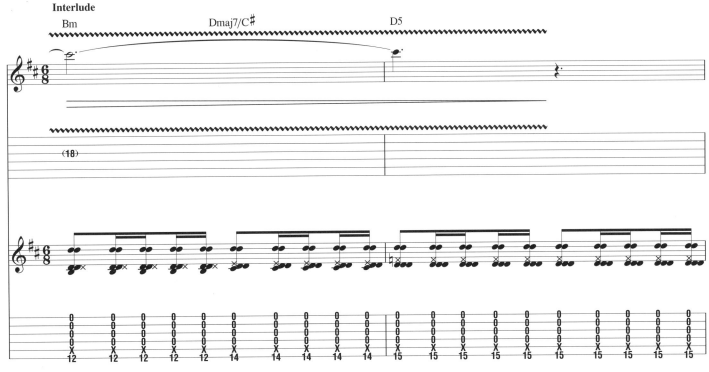

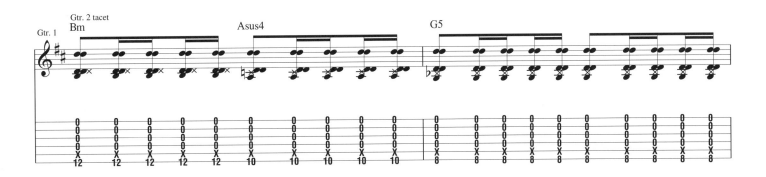

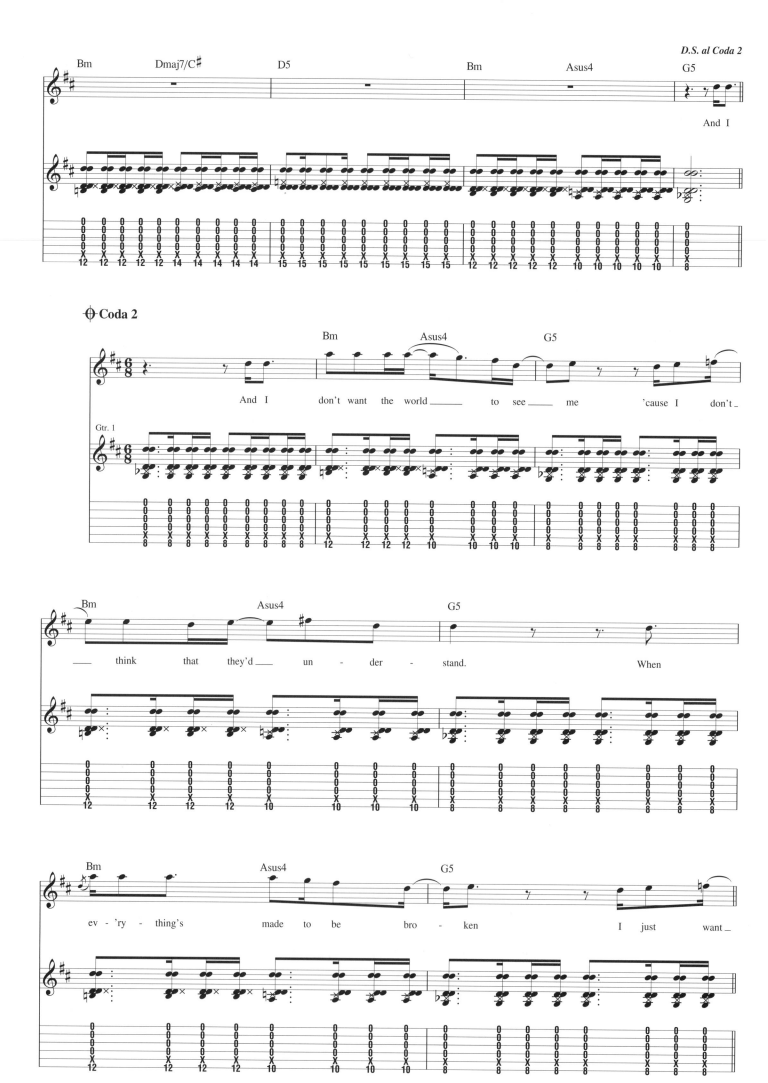

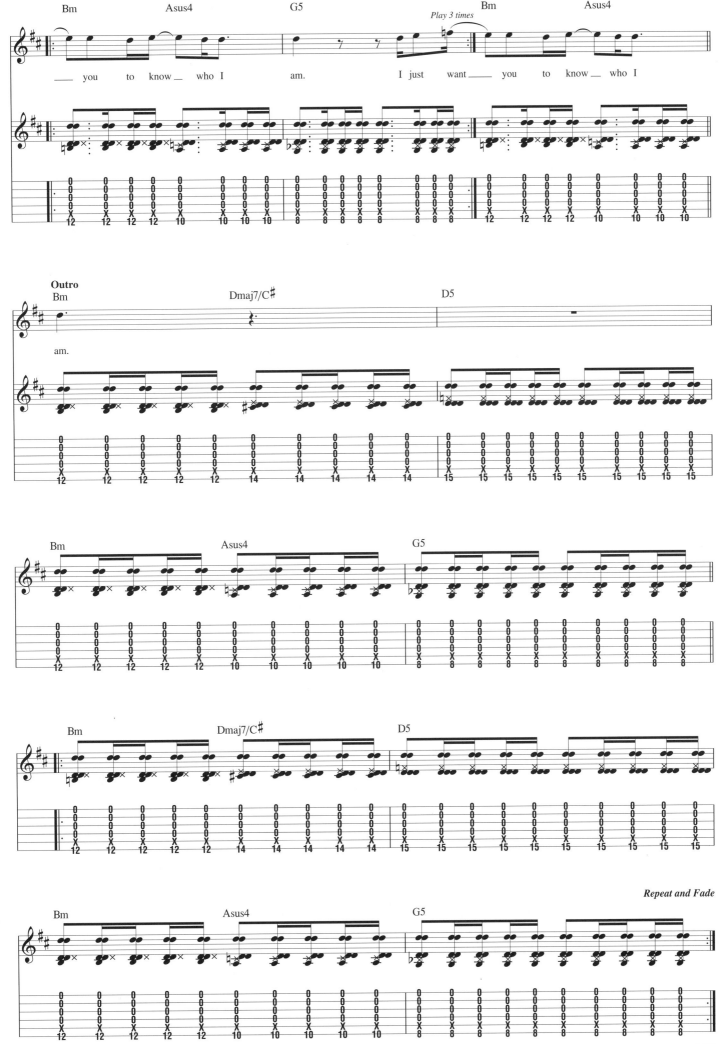

Jane Says

Words and Music by Perry Farrell, Dave Navarro, Stephen Perkins and Eric Avery

Intro
Slowly ♩ = 88

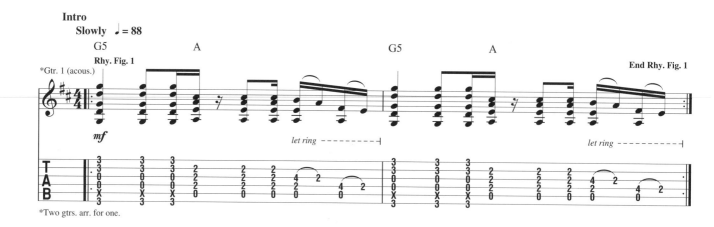

*Two gtrs. arr. for one.

Verse
Gtr. 1: w/ Rhy. Fig. 1 (6 times)

1. Jane says, "I'm done with Serg - i - o;___ he treat me like___ a rag_____
2. Jane says, "Have you seen my wig a - round?_ I feel na - ked___ with - out_

*Vocals doubled in unison throughout except where harmonies are indicated.

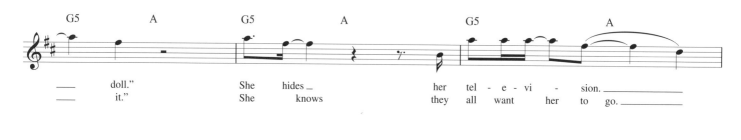

___ doll." She hides___ her tel - e - vi - sion._____
___ it." She knows they all want her to go.___

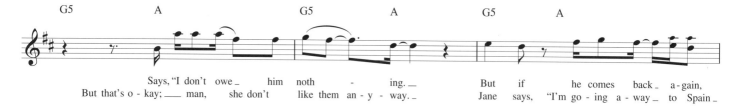

Says, "I don't owe___ him noth - ing.___ But if he comes back___ a - gain,
But that's o - kay;___ man, she don't like them an - y - way.___ Jane says, "I'm go - ing a - way___ to Spain___

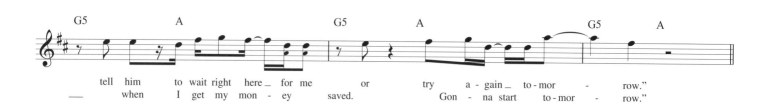

tell him to wait right here___ for me or try a - gain___ to - mor - row."
___ when I get my mon - ey saved. Gon - na start to - mor - row."

%. Chorus

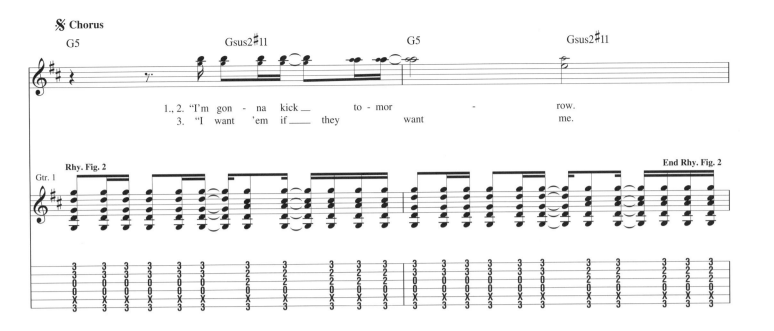

1., 2. "I'm gon - na kick ___ to - mor - row.
3. "I want 'em if ___ they want ___ me.

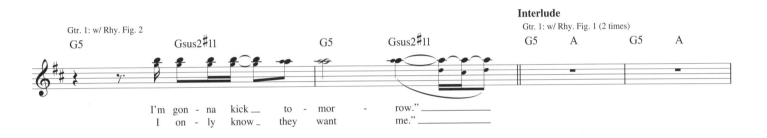

Interlude

I'm gon - na kick ___ to - mor - row." ___
I on - ly know ___ they want ___ me." ___

Verse

3., 5. She gets mad ___ and she starts to cry. ___ She

takes a ___ swing, ___ man. She can't hit! She don't ___

117

1st time, Gtr. 1: w/ Rhy. Fig. 1 (2 times)
2nd time, Gtr. 1: w/ Rhy. Fig. 1 (2 1/2 times)

mean no ___ harm; ___ she just ___ don't _____ know ___ (Don't know, don't know.) what else to do ___ a - bout ___

Verse

Gtr. 1: w/ Rhy. Fig. 1 (6 times)

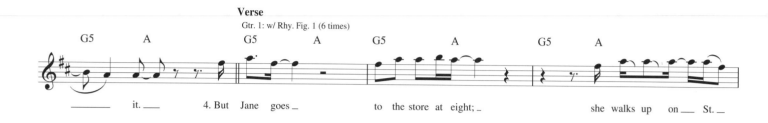

_____ it. ___ 4. But Jane goes ___ to the store at eight; ___ she walks up on ___ St. ___

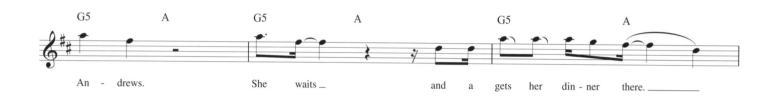

An - drews. She waits ___ and a gets her din - ner there. _____

She pulls her din - ner from her pock - et. ___ Jane says, "I ain't ___ nev - er been ___ in

D.S. al Coda

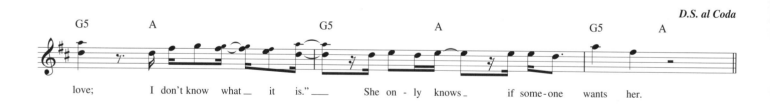

love; I don't know what ___ it is." ___ She on - ly knows ___ if some - one wants her.

⊕ **Coda**

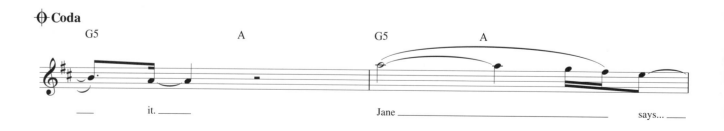

___ it. _____ Jane _____ says... ___

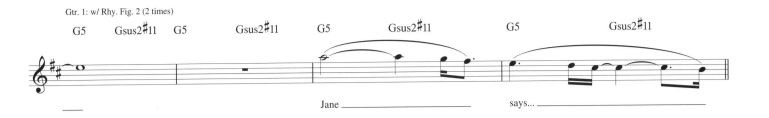

Gtr. 1: w/ Rhy. Fig. 2 (2 times)

G5   Gsus2#11   G5   Gsus2#11   G5   Gsus2#11   G5   Gsus2#11

Jane _____ says...

Outro

Gtr. 1: w/ Rhy. Fig. 1 (4 1/2 times)

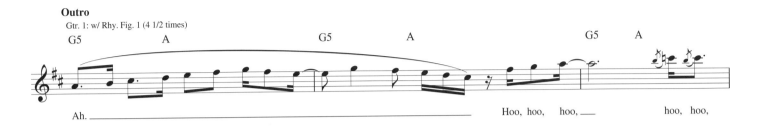

G5   A   G5   A   G5   A

Ah. _____ Hoo, hoo, hoo, ____   hoo, hoo,

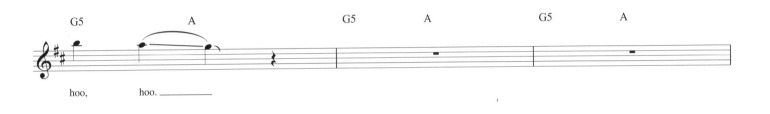

G5   A   G5   A   G5   A

hoo,   hoo. _____

G5   A   G5   A   G5   A

Begin fade

Gtr. 1: w/ Rhy. Fig. 2 (2 times)

G5   Gsus2#11   G5   Gsus2#11   G5   Gsus2#11

Fade out

Gtr. 1: w/ Rhy. Fig. 1

G5   Gsus2#11   G5   A   G5   A

The Joker

Words and Music by Steve Miller, Eddie Curtis and Ahmet Ertegun

Gtrs. 1, 2 & 4: Tune down 1 step:
(low to high) D-G-C-F-A-D

Gtr. 3: Open E tuning, down 1 step:
(low to high) D-A-D-F♯-A-D

Intro
Moderately slow ♩ = 88

*Chord symbols reflect overall harmony.

pick - er,   I'm a grin - ner,   I'm a lov - er, ___ and I'm a sin - ner.

I play my mu - sic in ___ the sun. ___ I'm a

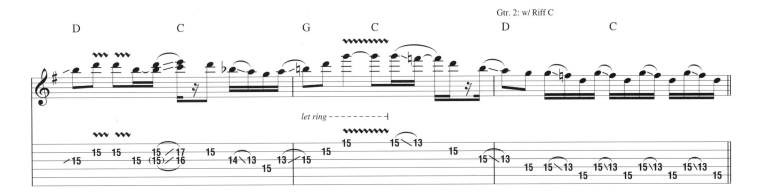

Verse

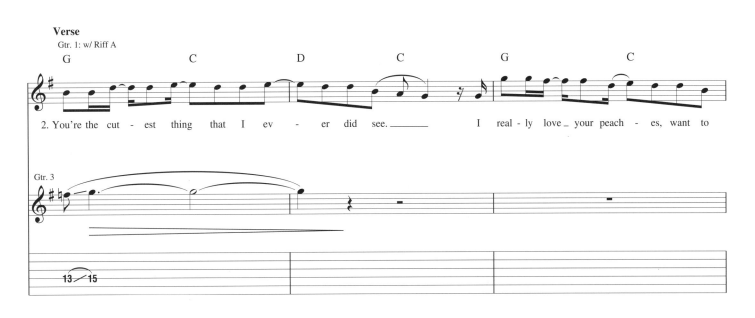

2. You're the cut - est thing that I ev - er did see. ___ I real - ly love _ your peach - es, want to

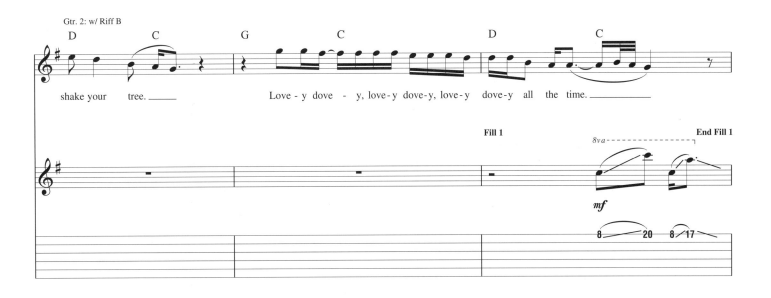

shake your tree. ___ Love - y dove - y, love-y dove-y, love-y dove-y all the time. ___

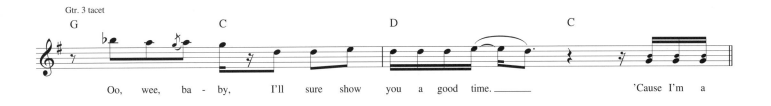

Oo, wee, ba - by, I'll sure show you a good time. ___ 'Cause I'm a

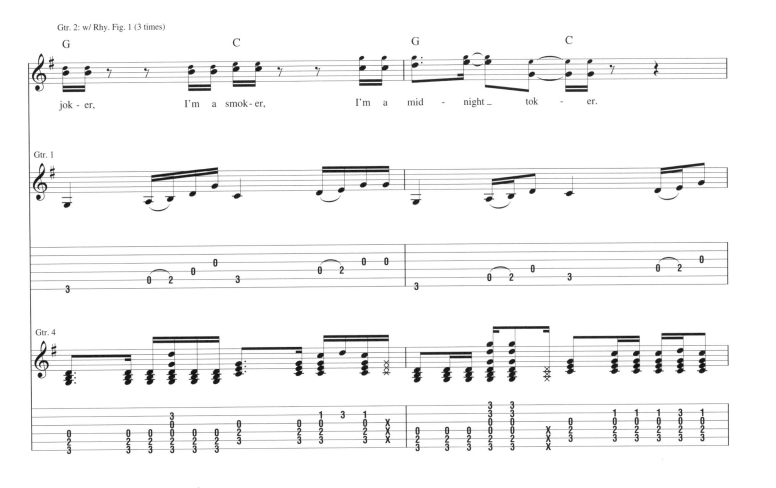

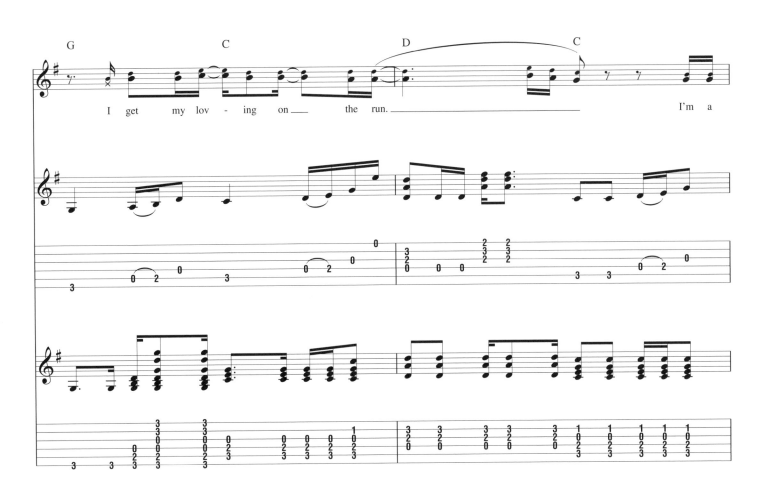

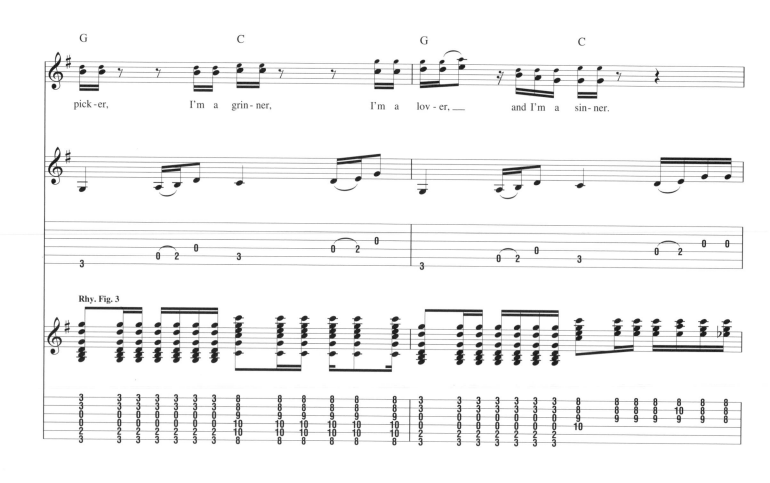

pick-er,   I'm a grin-ner,   I'm a lov-er, ___   and I'm a sin-ner.

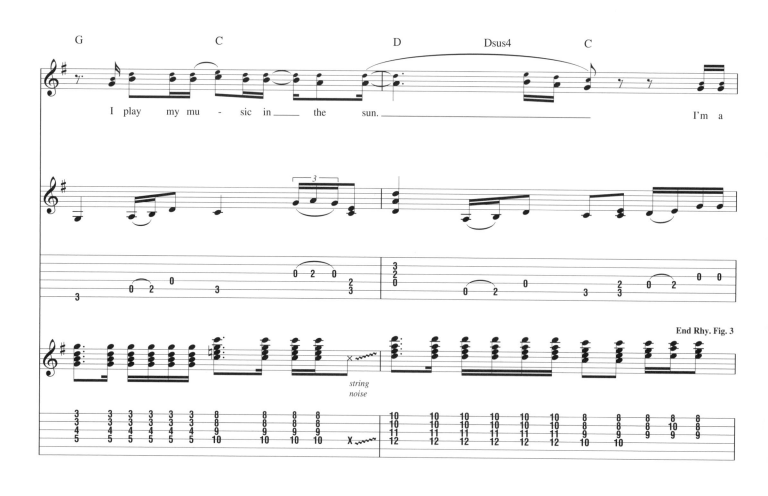

I play my mu - sic in ___ the sun. _____ I'm a

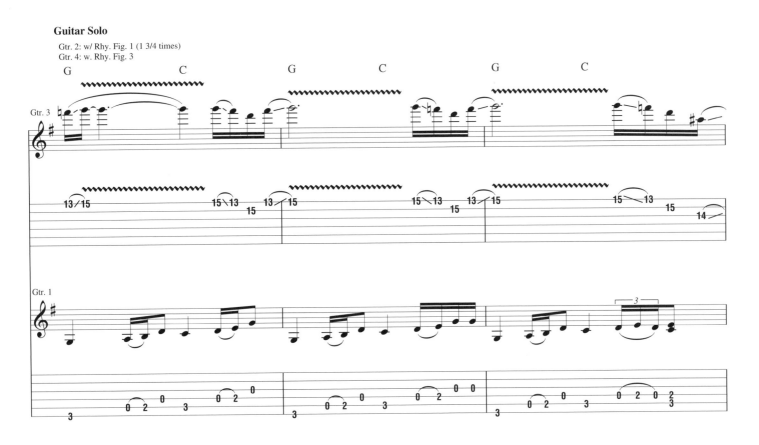

Outro-Verse

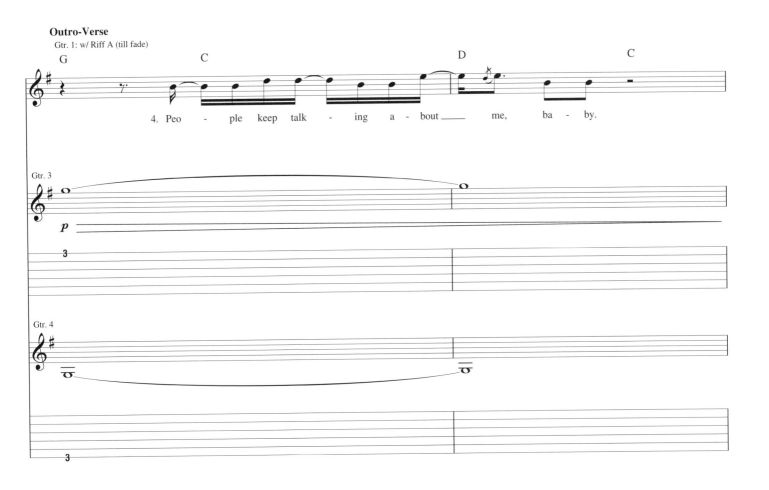

4. Peo - ple keep talk - ing a - bout _____ me, ba - by.

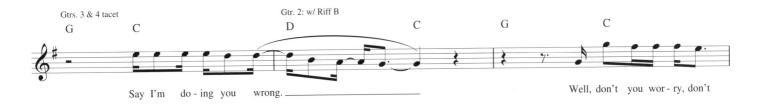

Say I'm do - ing you wrong. _____ Well, don't you wor - ry, don't

wor - ry, no don't wor - ry, ma - ma, _____ 'cause I'm right here at home. _____

Landslide

Words and Music by Stevie Nicks

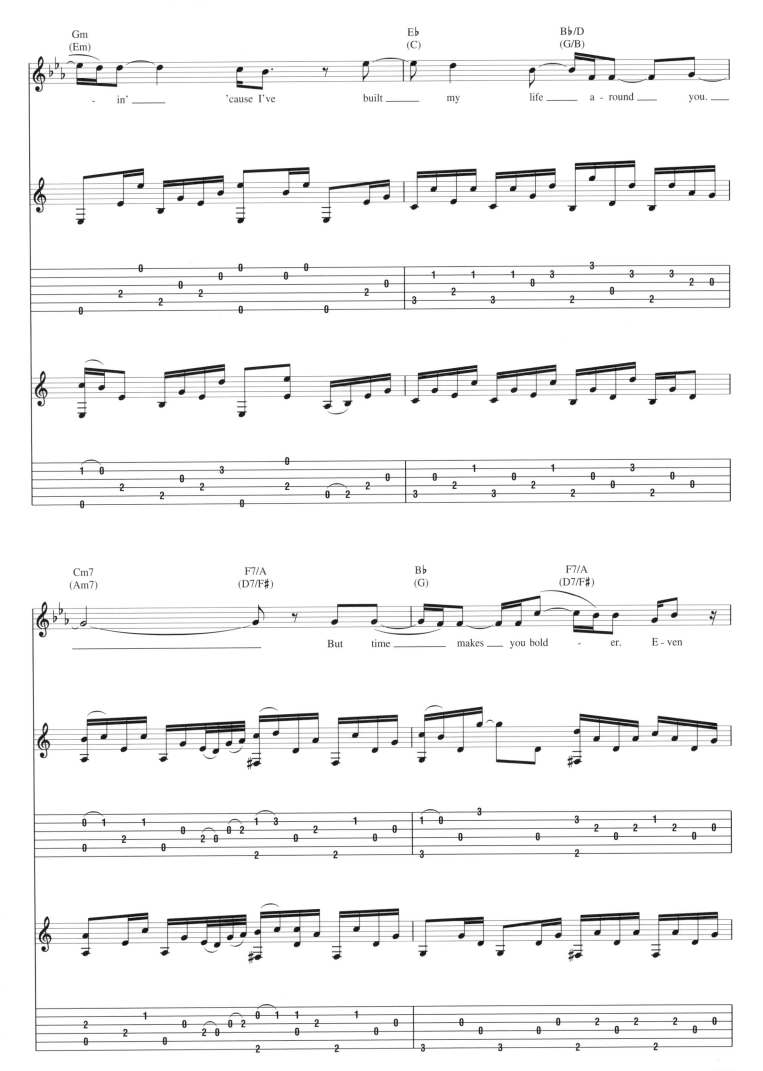

chil - dren _ get old - er _ and I'm _____ get-tin' old - er _____ too. _____

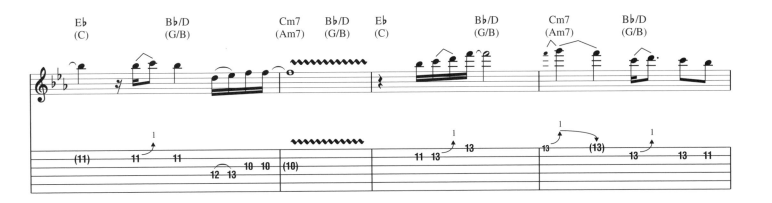

140

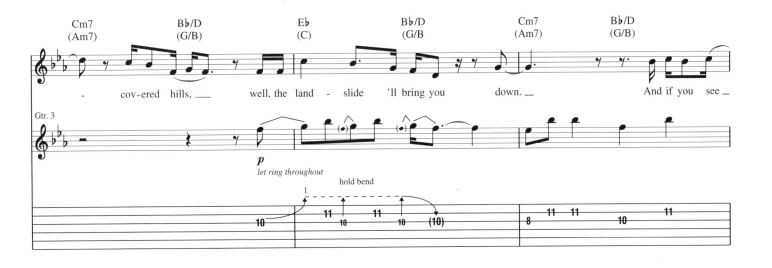

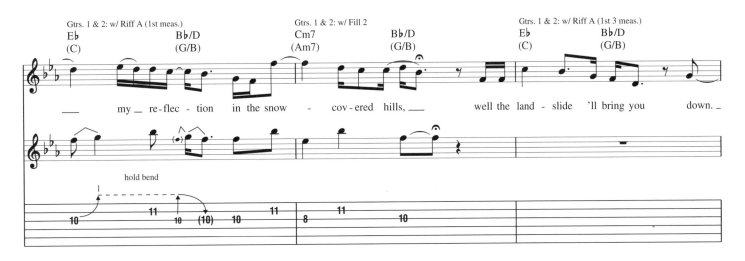

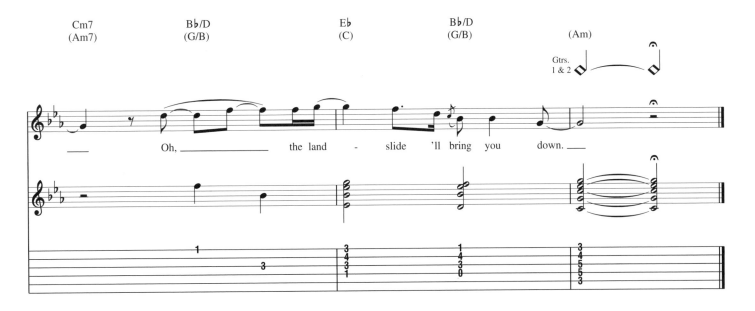

Like the Way I Do

Words and Music by Melissa Etheridge

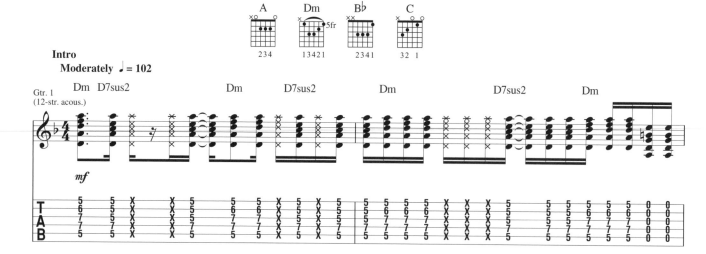

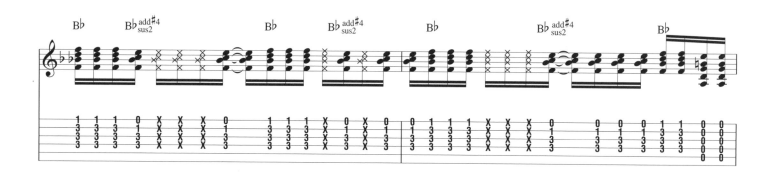

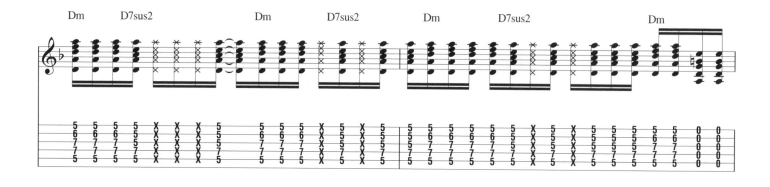

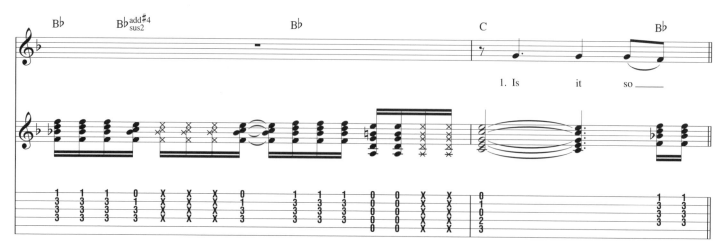

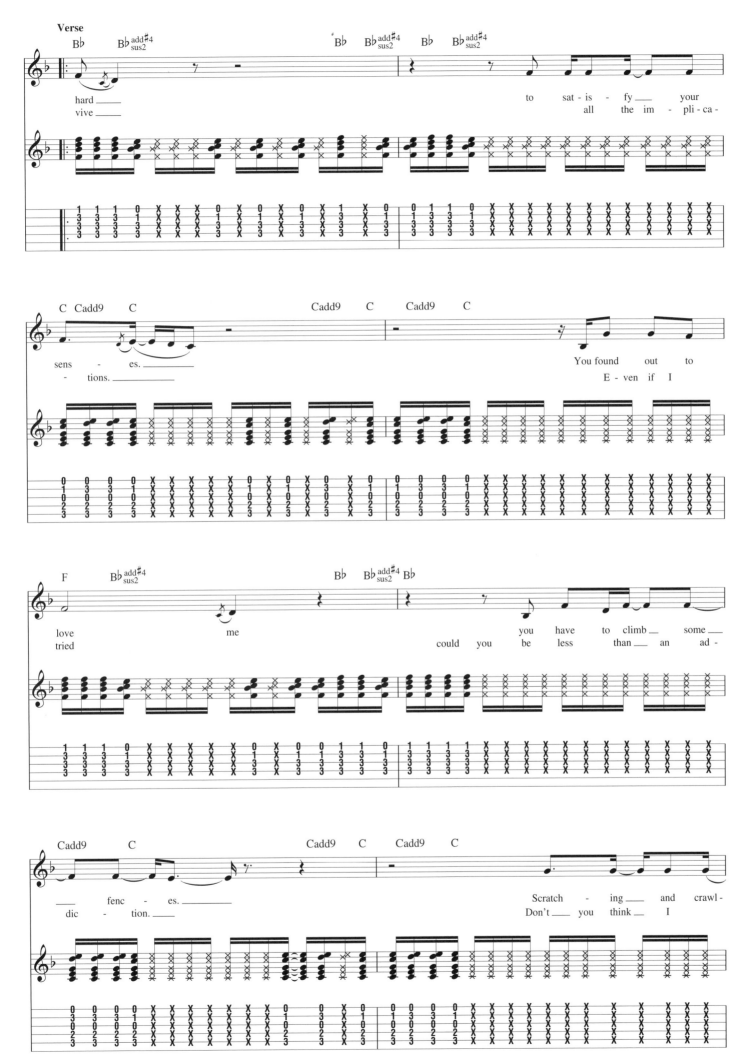

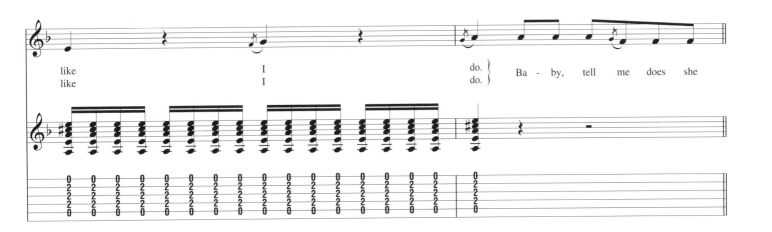

like   I   do.   Ba - by, tell me does she
like   I   do.

Chorus

love you   like the way   I   love you.   Does she stim - u - late

Gtr. 1   Rhy. Fig. 1

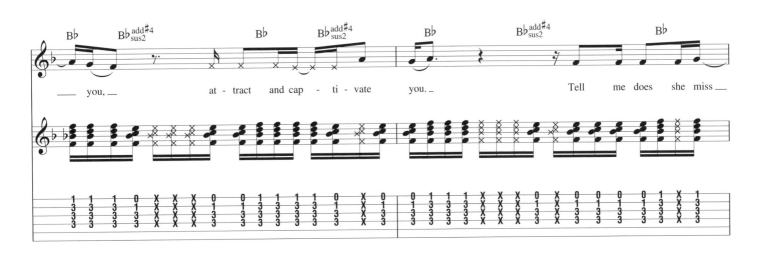

    you,   at - tract and cap - ti - vate you.   Tell me does she miss

    you,   ex - ist - ing just to kiss   you,   like the way I

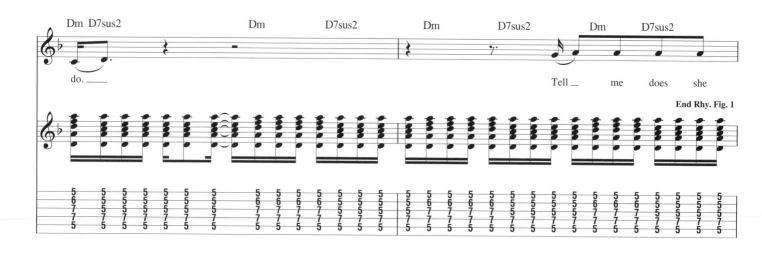

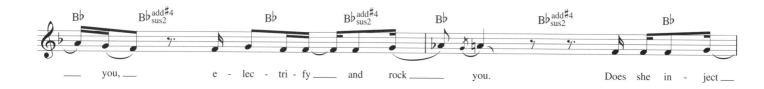

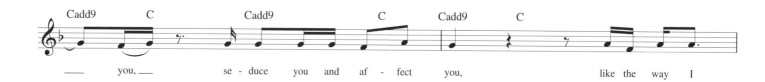

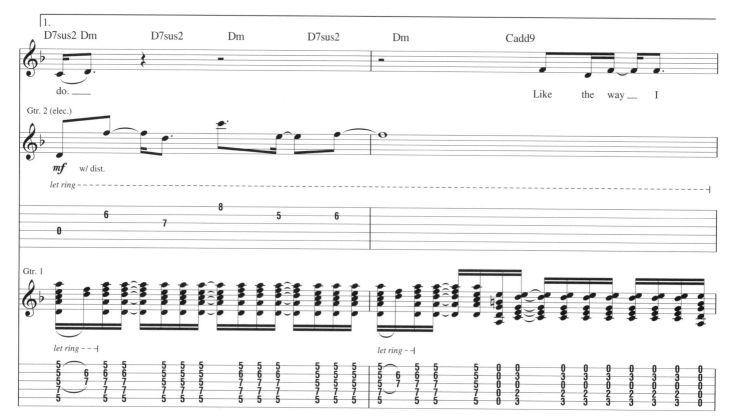

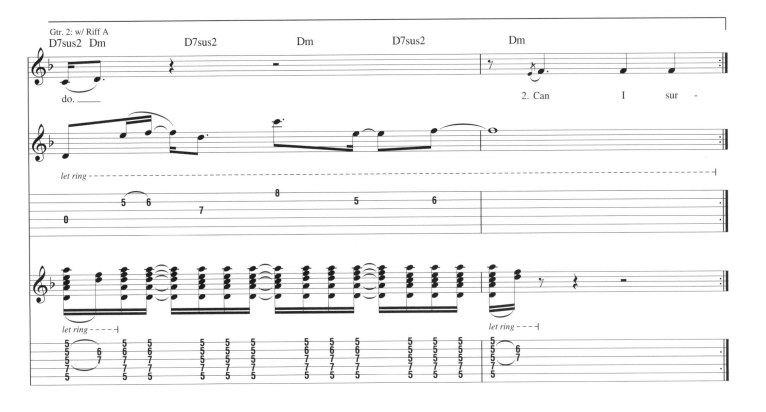

147

Outro-Guitar Solo

Love the One You're With

Words and Music by Stephen Stills

Open E5 tuning, down 2 steps:
(low to high) C-C↓-C-C↓-G-C

Intro
Moderately ♩ = 97

*Gtr. 1 (12-str. acous.)

let ring throughout

**Chord symbols reflect overall harmony (relative to detuned guitars).

*Three gtrs. arr. for one.

1. If you're down ___

Verse

Gtr. 1: w/ Rhy. Fig. 1 (4 times)

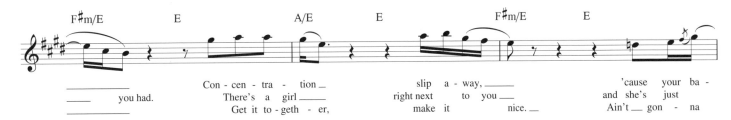

gry, —	and con-fused, ___	and you don't re-mem-ber ___	who you're talk-in' to. ___
ache	don't be sad, ___	and don't sit cry-in'	o-ver good times ___
	right in-to joy. ___	She is a girl, ___	and you're — a boy. ___

___ you had.	Con-cen-tra-tion ___	slip a-way, ___	'cause your ba-
	There's a girl ___	right next to you ___	and she's just
	Get it to-geth-er,	make it nice. ___	Ain't ___ gon-na

- by _____ is so far a - way. _____
wait - in' ___ for some - thin' to do. ___ Well,
need _____ an - y more ad - vice. _____ And } there's a rose
And

Pre-Chorus

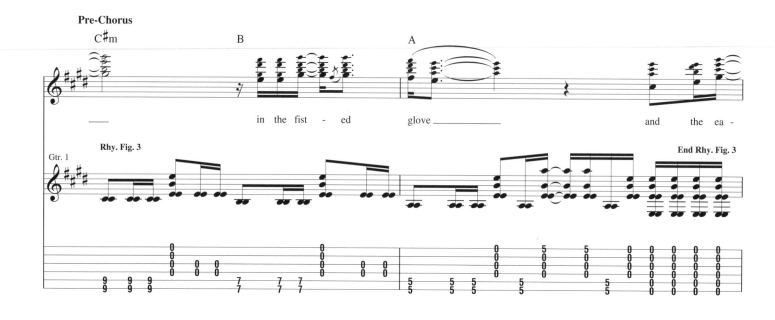

___ in the fist - ed glove _____ and the ea -

Gtr. 1: w/ Rhy. Fig. 3 (2 times)

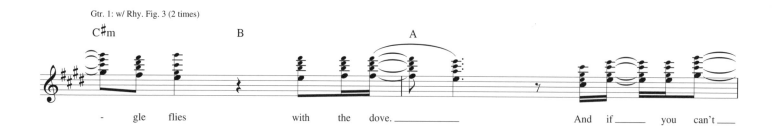

- gle flies with the dove. ___ And if ___ you can't ___

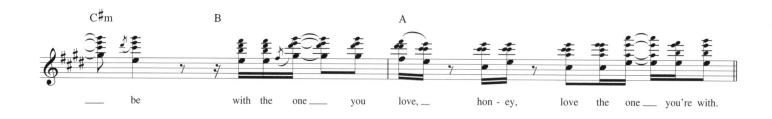

___ be with the one ___ you love, ___ hon - ey, love the one ___ you're with.

Chorus

To Coda ⊕

Gtr. 1: w/ Rhy. Fig. 1

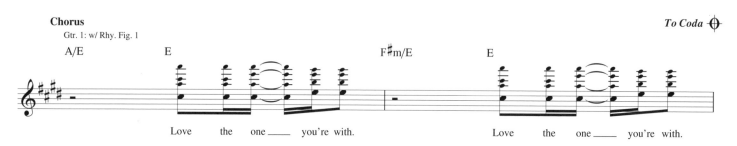

Love the one ___ you're with. Love the one ___ you're with.

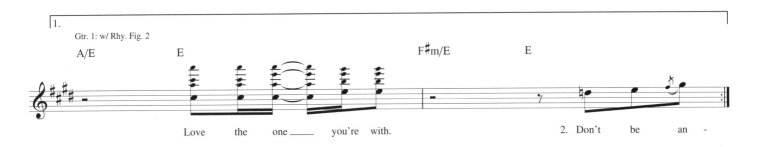

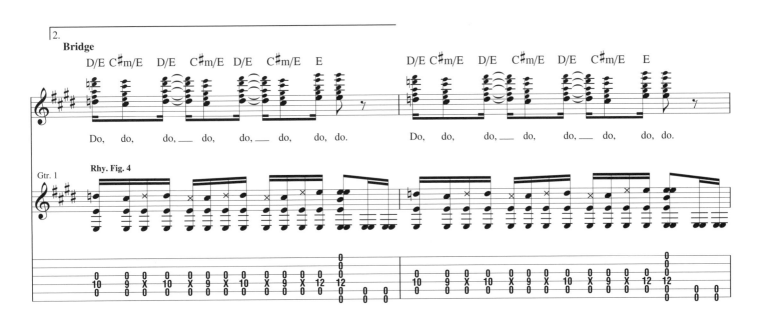

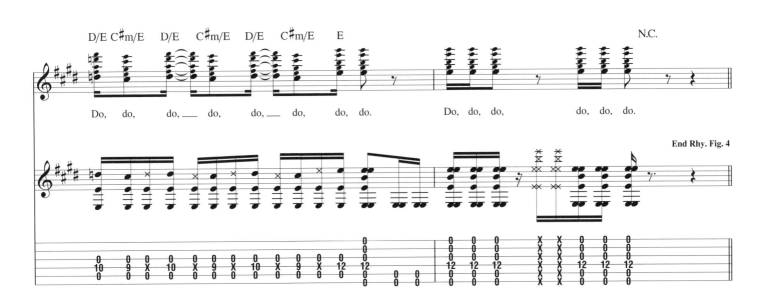

Organ Solo

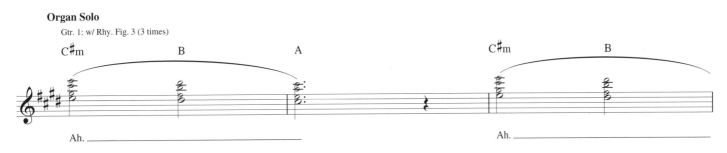

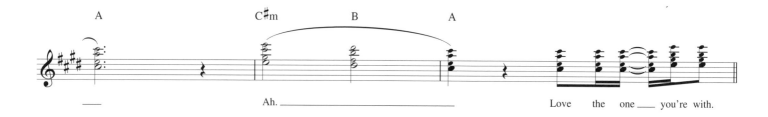

A — C#m — B — A

Ah._____ Love the one ___ you're with.

Chorus

Gtr. 1: w/ Rhy. Fig. 1

A/E   E   F#m/E   E

Love the one ___ you're with.   Love the one ___ you're with.

D.S. al Coda

Gtr. 1: w/ Rhy. Fig. 2

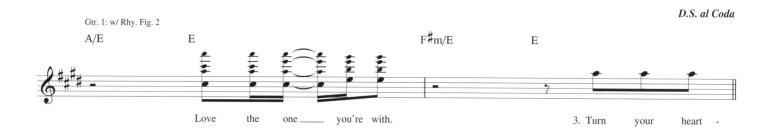

A/E   E   F#m/E   E

Love the one ___ you're with.   3. Turn your heart-

⊕ Coda

Gtr. 1: w/ Rhy. Fig. 2

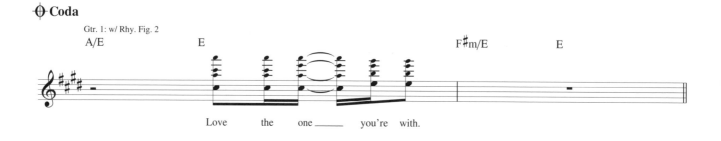

A/E   E   F#m/E   E

Love the one ___ you're with.

Outro

Gtr. 1: w/ Rhy. Fig. 4

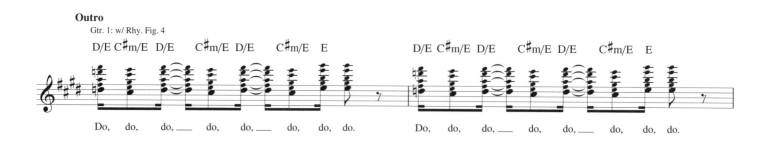

D/E C#m/E D/E   C#m/E D/E   C#m/E E   D/E C#m/E D/E   C#m/E D/E   C#m/E E

Do, do, do,___ do, do,___ do, do, do.   Do, do, do,___ do, do,___ do, do, do.

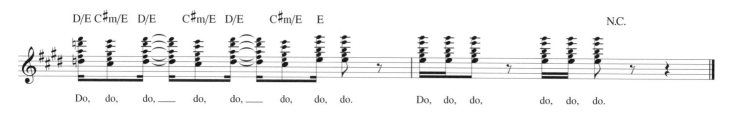

D/E C#m/E D/E   C#m/E D/E   C#m/E E   N.C.

Do, do, do,___ do, do,___ do, do, do.   Do, do, do,   do, do, do.

Maggie May

Words and Music by Rod Stewart and Martin Quittenton

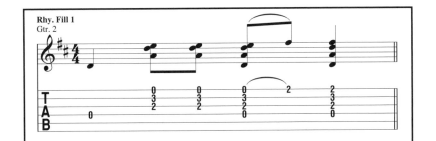

Guitar Solo

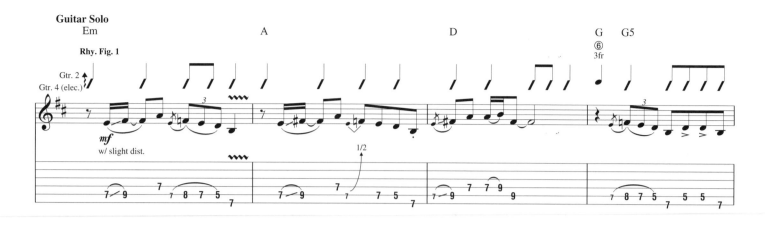

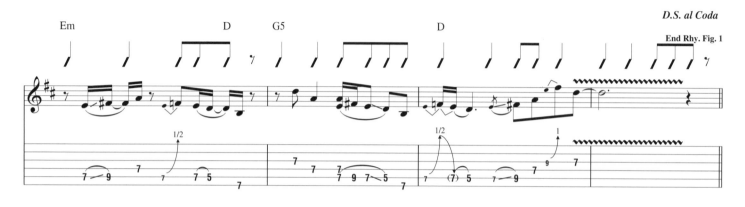

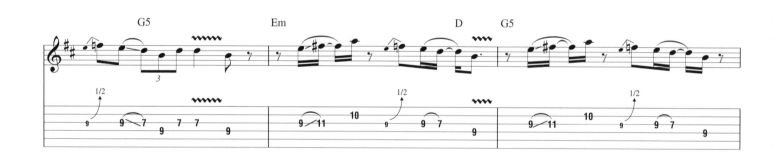

160

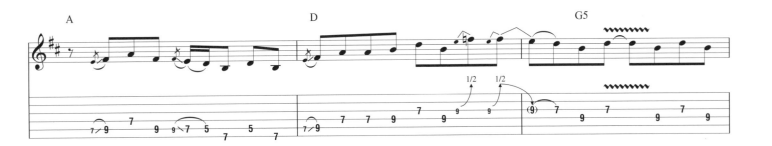

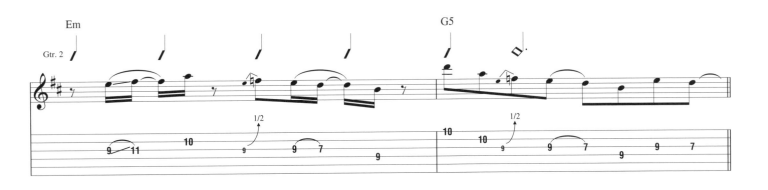

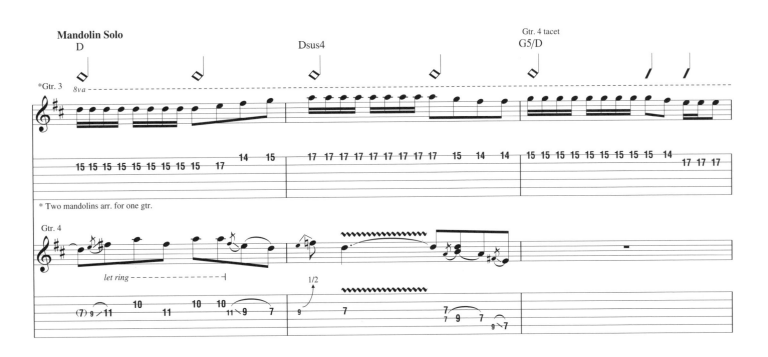

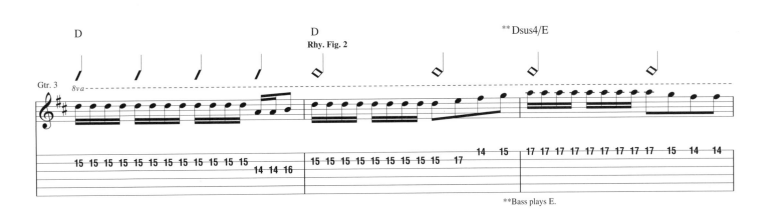

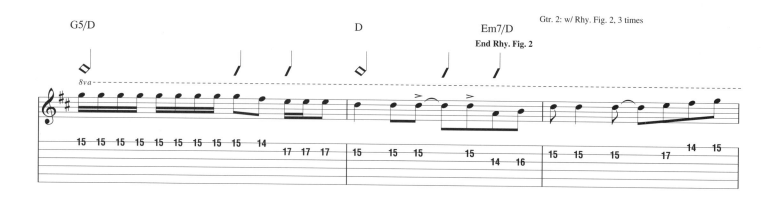

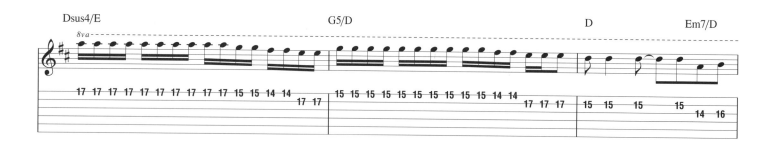

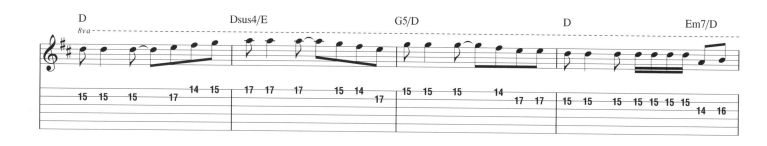

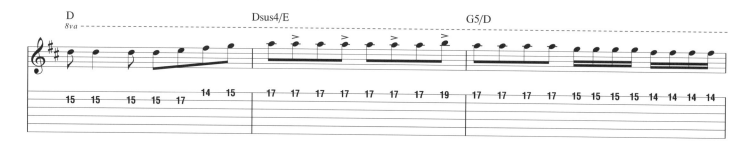

Outro

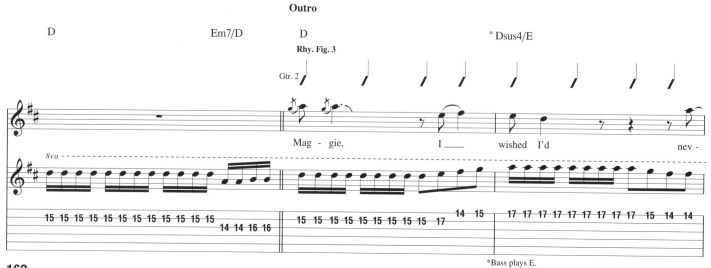

Mag - gie, I ___ wished I'd nev-

*Bass plays E.

162

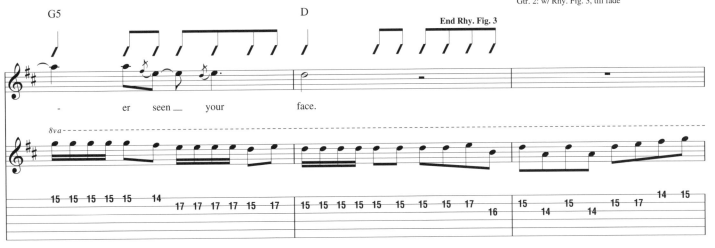

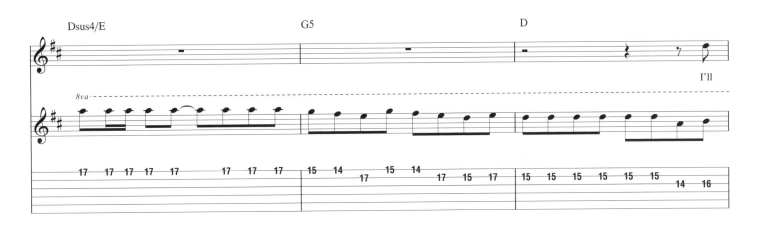

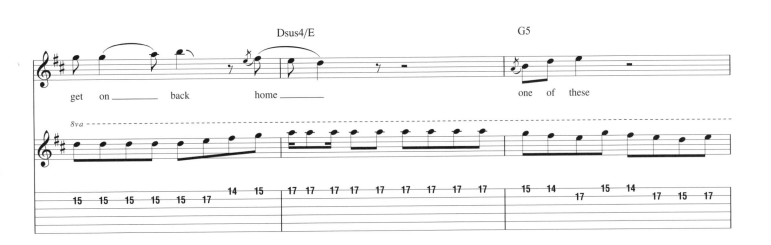

days. _____ Whoo, whoo. _____

Additional Lyrics

4. I suppose I could collect my books and get back to school,
    Or steal my daddy's cue and make a living out of playing pool,
    Or find myself a rock and roll band that needs a helping hand.
    Oh Maggie, I wished I'd never seen your face.
    You made a first class fool out of me,
    But I was blind as a fool can be.
    You stole my heart, but I love you anyway.

Melissa

Words and Music by Gregg Allman and Steve Alaimo

Gtr. 1: w/Fill 2, 2nd time
Gtr. 1: w/Fill 4, 3rd time

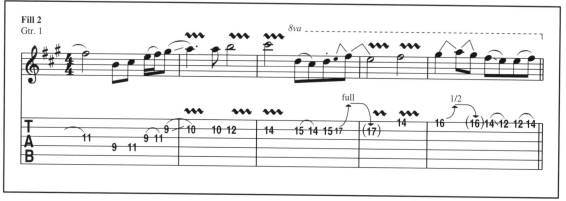

Fill 2
Gtr. 1

Fill 4
Gtr. 1

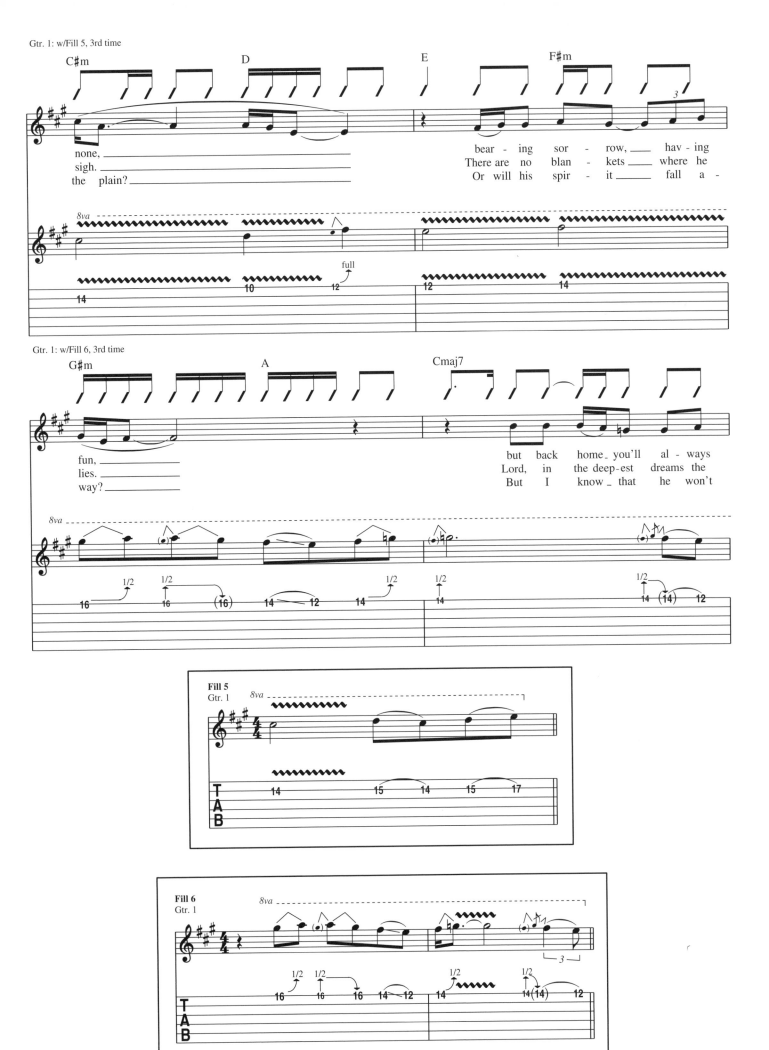

run   to   sweet   Mel - is - sa. _____
gypsy flies   with   sweet   Mel - is - sa. _____
stay   with - out   Mel - is - sa. _____

*volume swells w/volume pedal
or guitar's volume knob

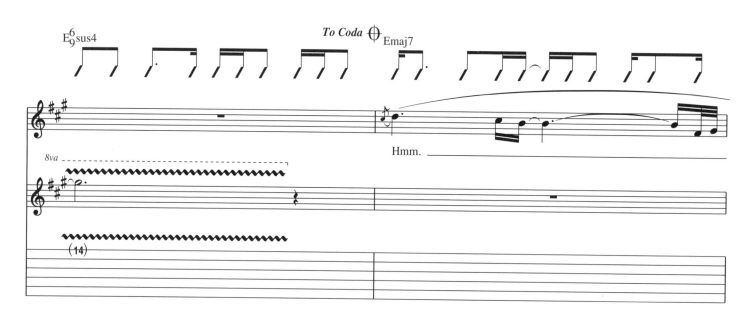

Hmm. _____

loco

Bridge

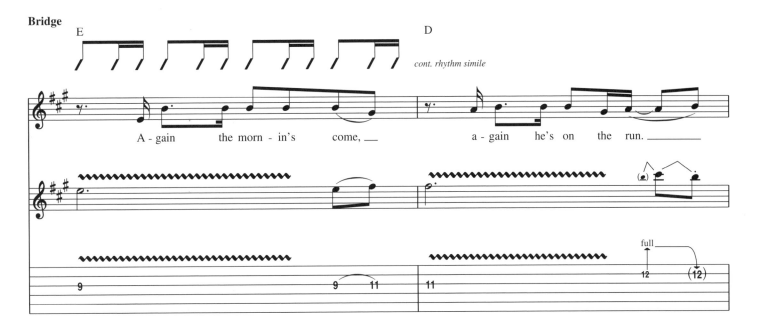

A - gain the morn - in's come, ___ a - gain he's on the run. _____

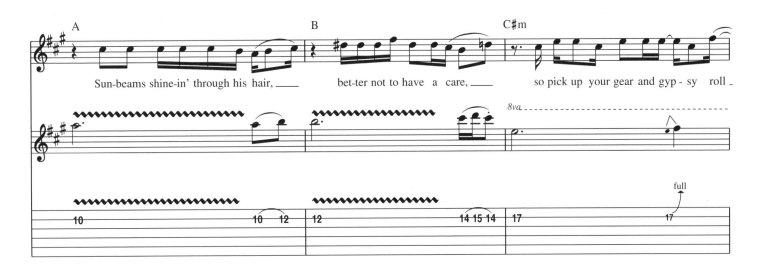

Sun-beams shine-in' through his hair, ___ bet-ter not to have a care, ___ so pick up your gear and gyp - sy roll

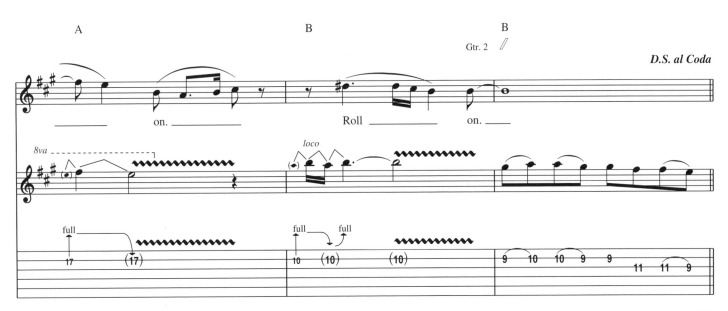

on. Roll _____ on. ___

Yes I know _ that he won't stay _ yeah, _____ with-out Mel - is - sa_____

Gtr. 2 cont. w/verse rhythm simile

*volume swells

No, no he just won't stay. ____ Mmm.

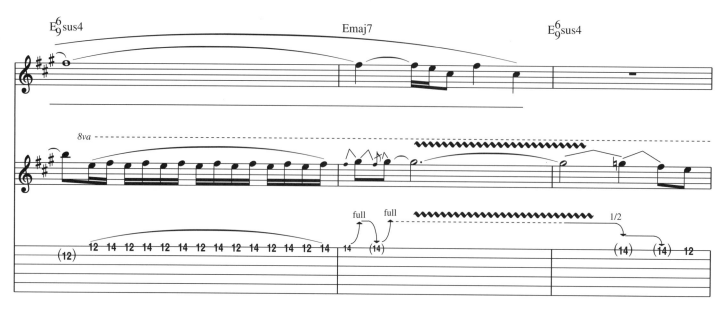

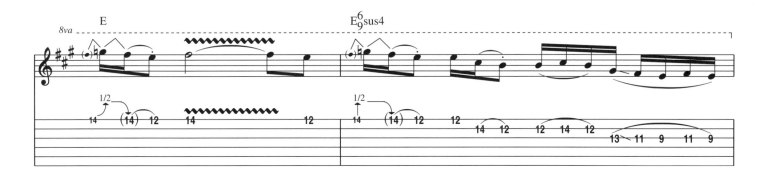

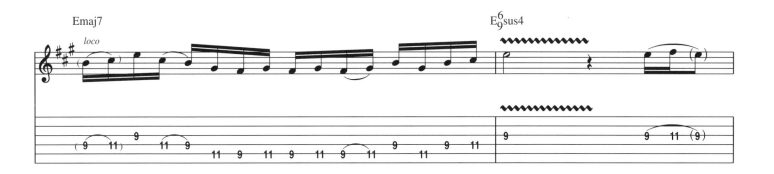

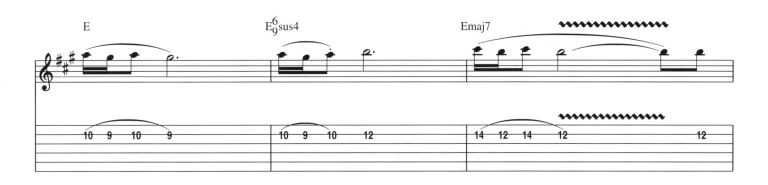

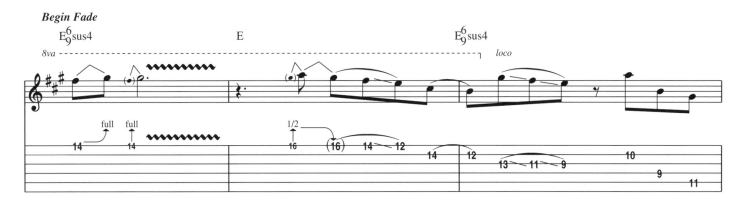

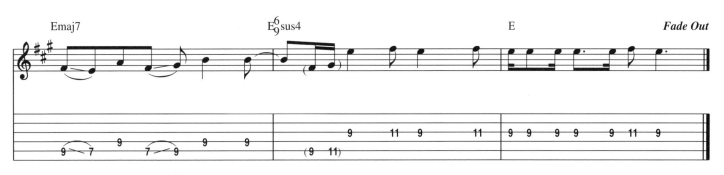

More Than Words

Words and Music by Nuno Bettencourt and Gary Cherone

Tune down 1/2 step:
(low to high) E♭-A♭-D♭-G♭-B♭-E♭

Intro

Moderately slow ♩ = 96

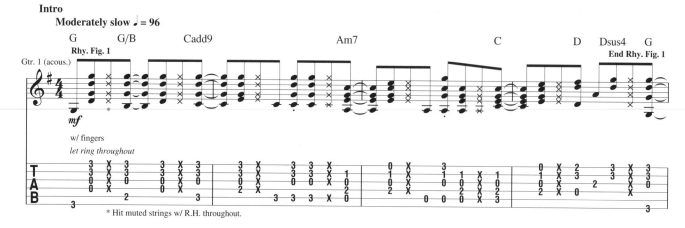

* Hit muted strings w/ R.H. throughout.

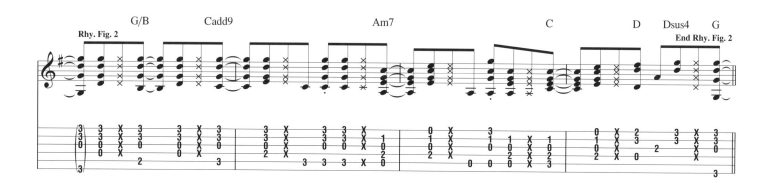

Verse

Gtr. 1: w/ Rhy. Fig. 2

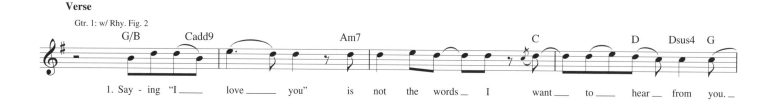

1. Say-ing "I ___ love ___ you" is not the words I want to ___ hear ___ from you. ___

It's not that I ___ want ___ you not to say, ___ but if ___

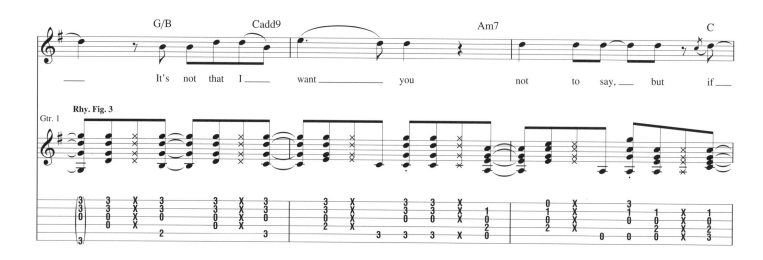

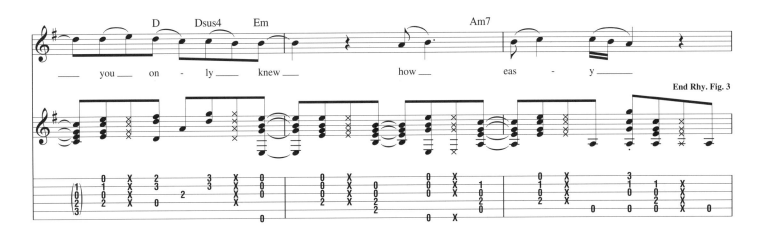

Chorus

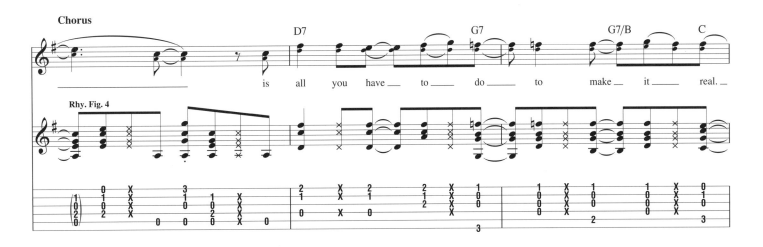

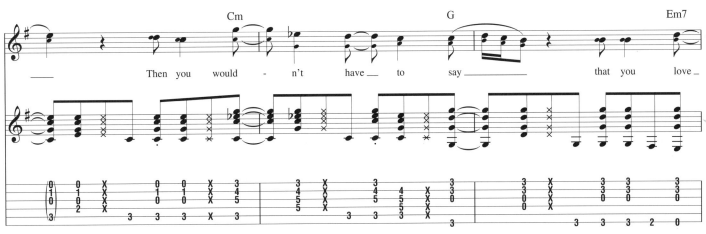

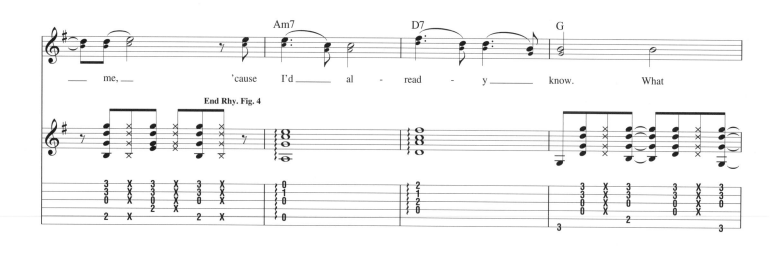

me, ___ 'cause I'd ___ al - read - y ___ know. What

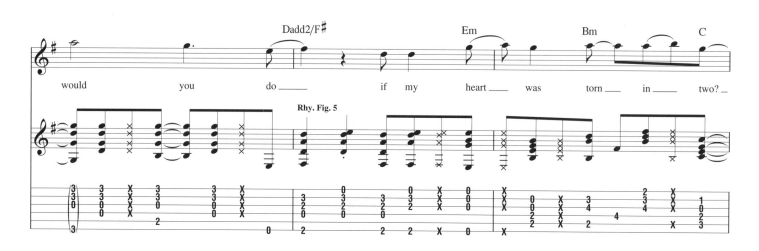

would you do ___ if my heart ___ was torn ___ in ___ two? ___

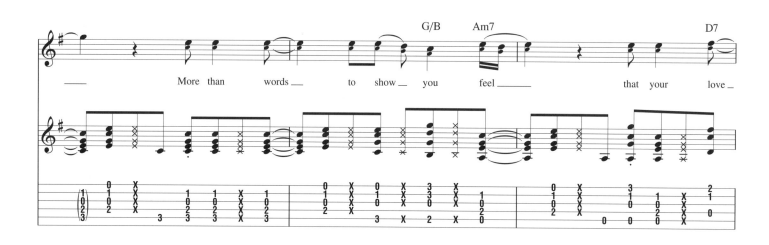

___ More than words ___ to show ___ you feel ___ that your love ___

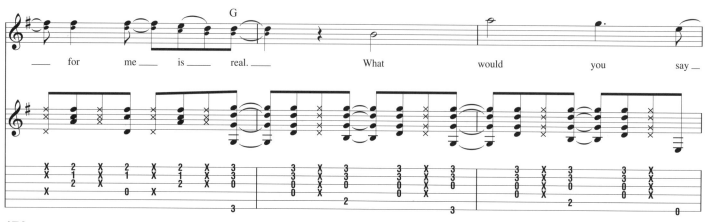

___ for me ___ is ___ real. What would you say ___

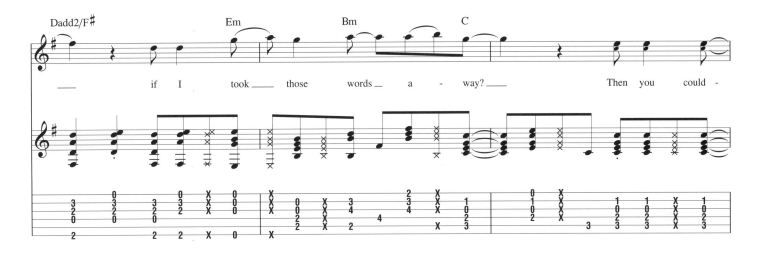

_if I took___ those words___ a - way?___ Then you could -_

_- n't make ___ things new ___ just by say - ing "I ___ love ___ you." ___ (You. ____

End Rhy. Fig. 5

Interlude

Gtr. 1: w/ Rhy. Fig. 1

_La, dee, da, ___ la, dee, da, ___ dee, dai, dai, da. ___ More ___ than ___ words. ____
_La, dee, da.) ____

_La, dee, da, ___ dai, ___ da. ____

Gtr. 1

* Hit body of gtr.

Verse

Gtr. 1: w/ Rhy. Fig. 1

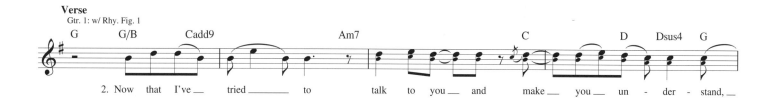

2. Now that I've ___ tried _____ to talk to you ___ and make ___ you un - der - stand, ___

Gtr. 1: w/ Rhy. Fig. 3

___ all ___ you have ___ to do ____ is close ___ your eyes ___ and just

reach out ____ your ___ hands ____ and touch ___ me. _____

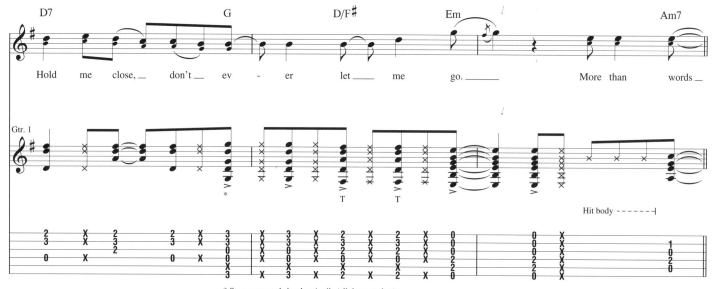

Hold me close, ___ don't ___ ev - er ___ let ___ me go. _____ More than words ___

Gtr. 1

* Strum accented chords w/ nails (all downstrokes);
hit muted strings w/ R.H. as before.

Chorus

Gtr. 1: w/ Rhy. Fig. 4

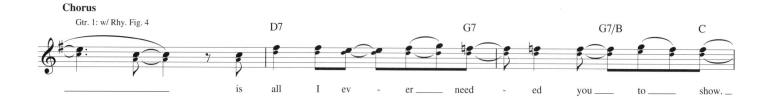

_____ is all I ev - er ___ need - ed you ___ to ___ show. ___

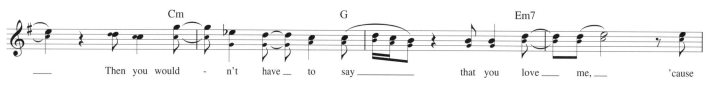

___ Then you would - n't have ___ to say _____ that you love ___ me, ___ 'cause

176

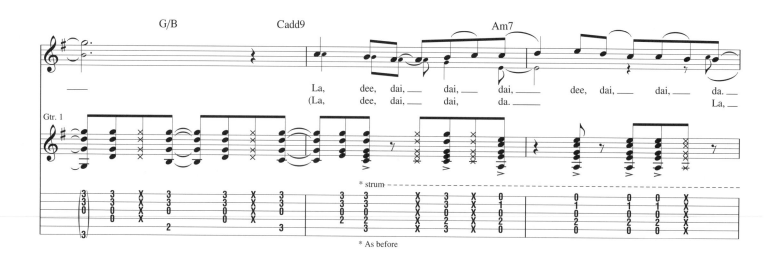

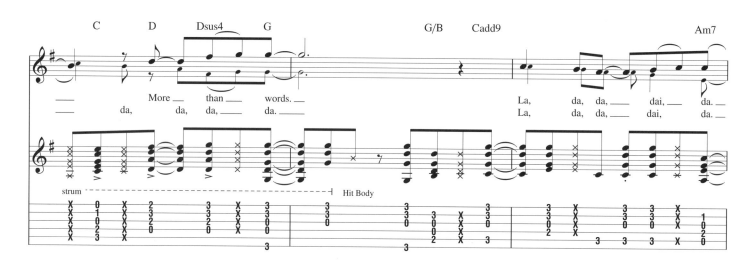

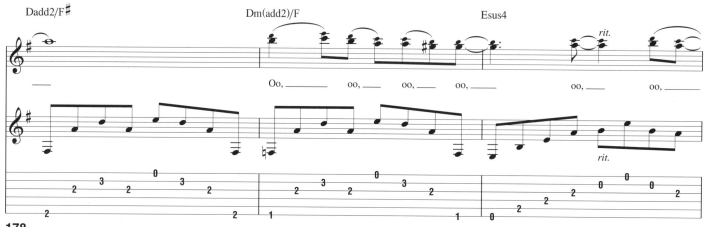

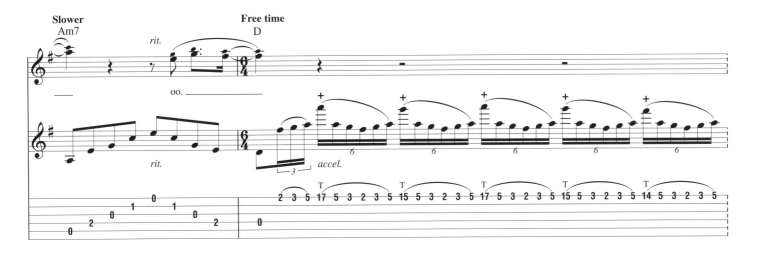

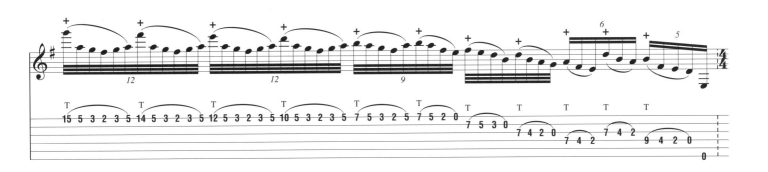

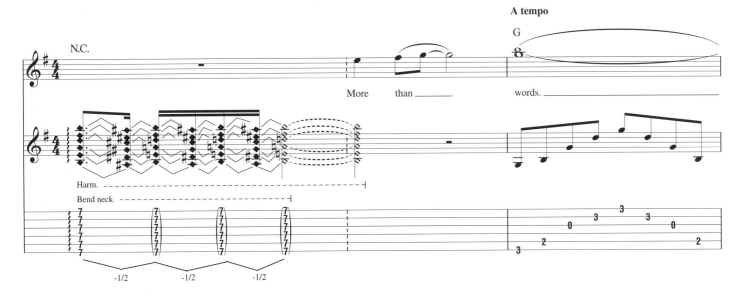

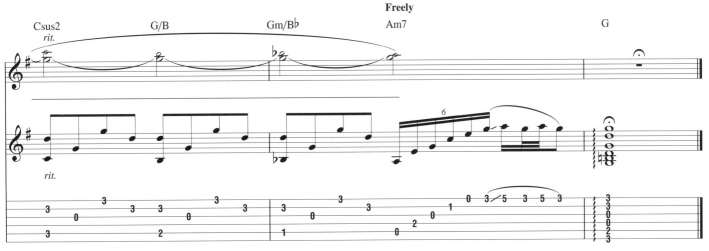

Norwegian Wood
(This Bird Has Flown)

Words and Music by John Lennon and Paul McCartney

All Gtrs.: Capo II

Intro

Moderately ♩. = 60

* Gtr. 1 (acous.)

(J.L.)

let ring throughout

* Notes tabbed at 2nd fret played as open strings.

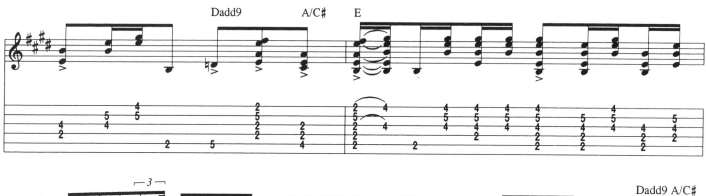

† Gtr. 2 (acous.)

† Gtr. 3 (acous.)

divisi

*Gtr. 4 (12 str. acous.)

† Sitar arr. for Gtrs. 2 & 3
* Notes tabbed at 2nd fret played as open strings.

wine.   We talked un - til ___ two,   and then she said,   "It's time for bed." ___

Interlude

Bridge
Gtrs. 2 & 3 tacet
Gtrs. 1 & 4: w/ Rhy. Figs. 2 & 2A

Em   A

told me she worked in the morn - ing and start - ed to laugh. __   I

Em   F#m7   B

told her I did-n't and crawled off to sleep in the bath. __

Verse
Gtrs. 1 & 4: w/ Rhy. Figs. 1 & 1A

E   Dadd9   A/C#

3. And when I a - woke I was a - lone, __ this bird had

Gtr. 2

Pink Houses

Words and Music by John Mellencamp

⊕ Coda

Chorus

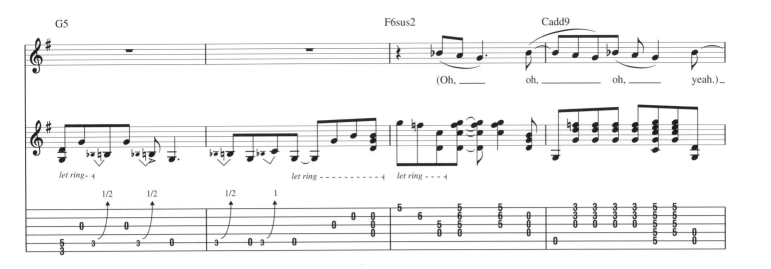

D.S. al Coda 2

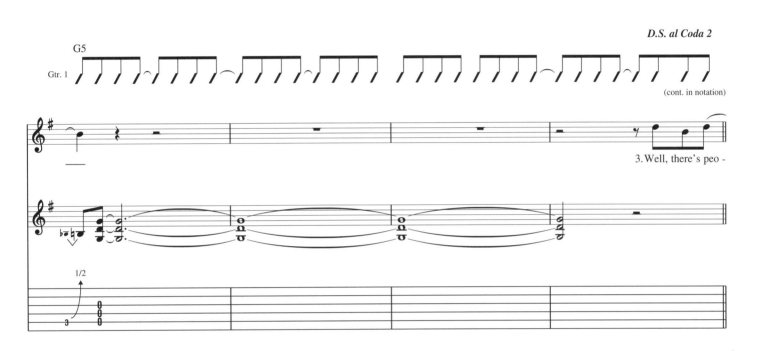

(cont. in notation)

3. Well, there's peo-

⊕ Coda 2

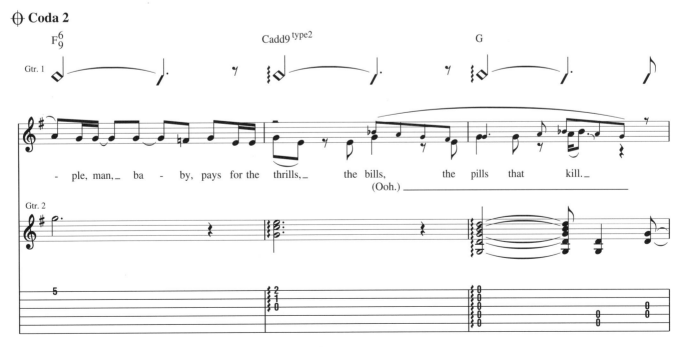

-ple, man,_ ba - by, pays for the thrills,_ the bills,_ the pills that kill._
(Ooh.) _____

Signs

Words and Music by Les Emmerson

*T = Thumb on ⑥

Bridge

say now, mis - ter, can't _ you read? You got to have a shirt and tie _ to get a seat. _

let ring

You can't watch, _ no, _ you _ can't _ eat. You ain't sup - posed to

be here. _ And the

sign said, "You got to have a mem-ber-ship card to get in - side." __ Ooh!

Guitar Solo

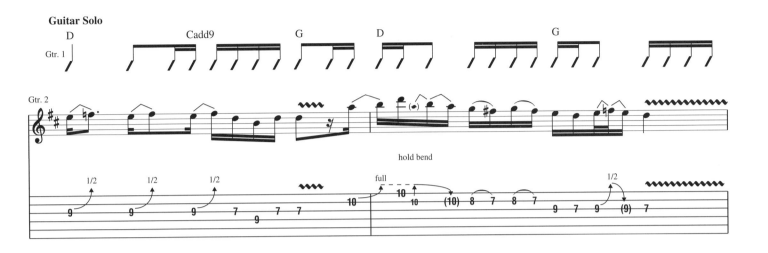

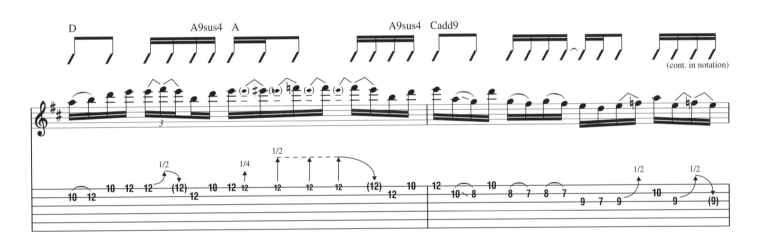

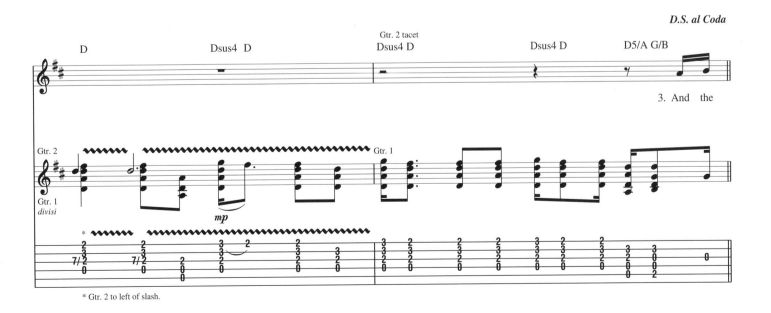

* Gtr. 2 to left of slash.

199

⊕ *Coda*

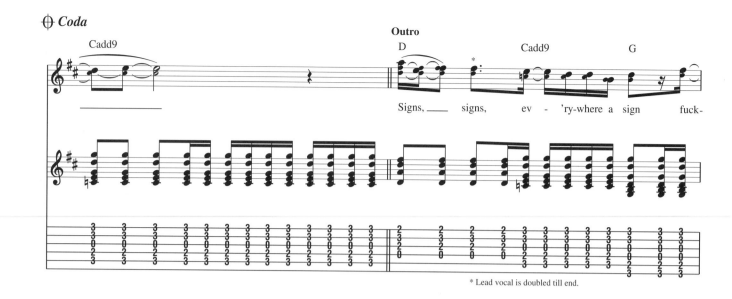

Outro

Signs, ___ signs, ev - 'ry-where a sign fuck-

* Lead vocal is doubled till end.

- ing up the scen - er - y, break - ing my mind. Do this, don't_ do ___ that. Can't you read _ the sign?

Additional Lyrics

2. And the sign says, "Anybody caught trespassing will be shot on sight."
   So I jumped the fence and yelled at the house, "Hey, what gives you the right
   To put up a fence to keep me out or to keep Mother Nature in?"
   If God was here he'd tell it to your face, "Man, you're some kinda sinner."

3. And the sign says, "Everybody welcome, come in and kneel down and pray."
   And then they pass around the plate at the end of it all, and I didn't have a penny to pay.
   So I got me a pen and paper, and I made up my own fuckin' sign.
   I said, "Thank you, Lord, for thinkin' about me, I'm alive and doing fine."

Silent Lucidity
Words and Music by Chris DeGarmo

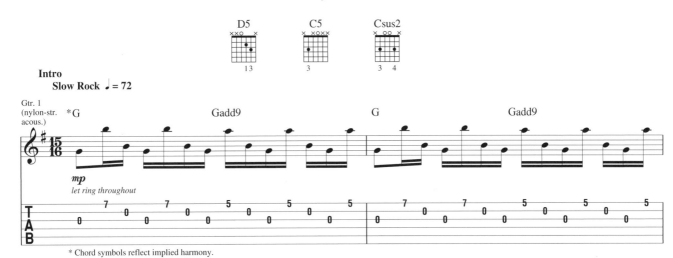

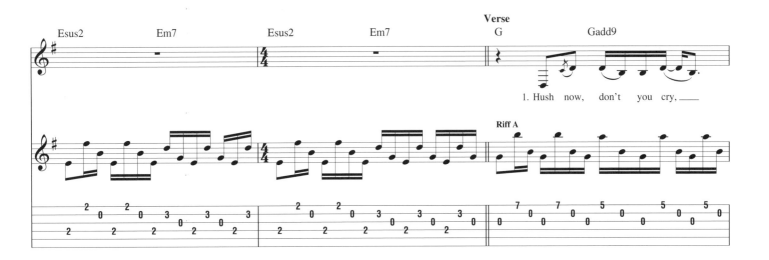

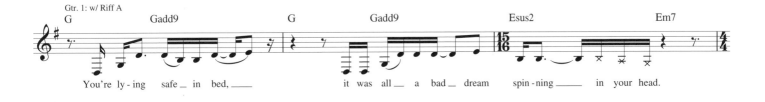

Your mind tricked you to feel _ the pain _ of some - one close _ to you _

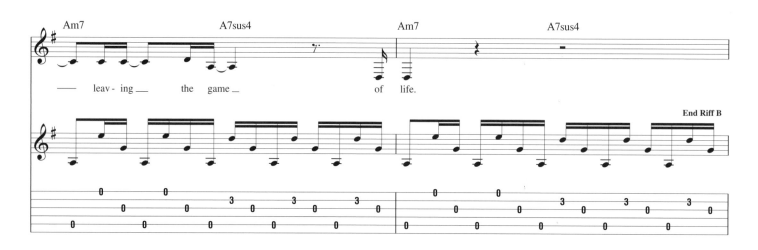

_ leav - ing _ the game _ of life.

So here it is, _ an - oth - er chance, _ wide a - wake _ you face _ the day, _ your dream is o - ver...

Interlude

or has it just be - gun?

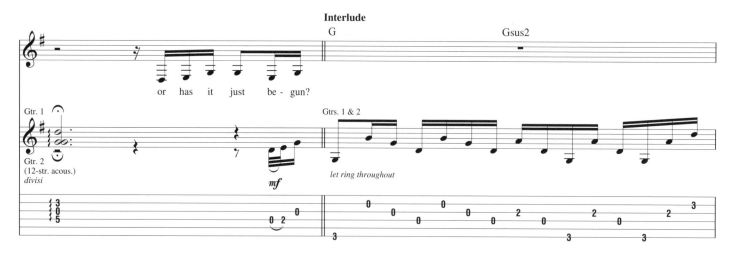

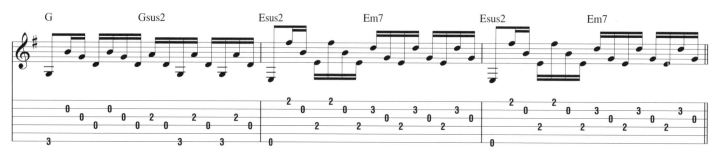

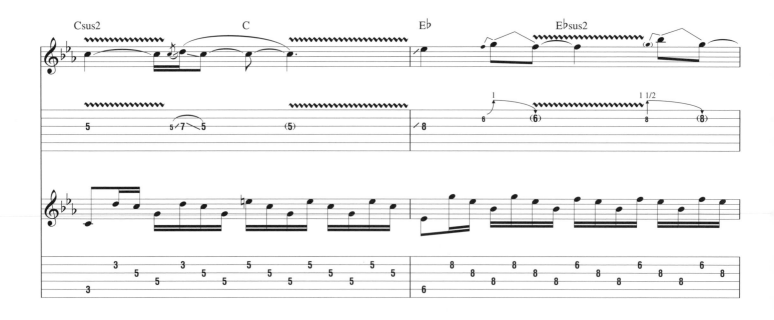

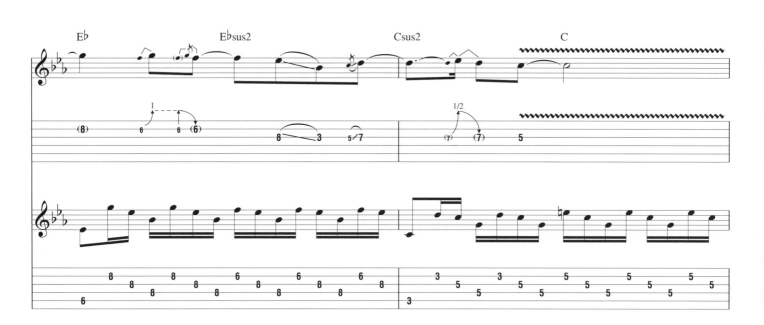

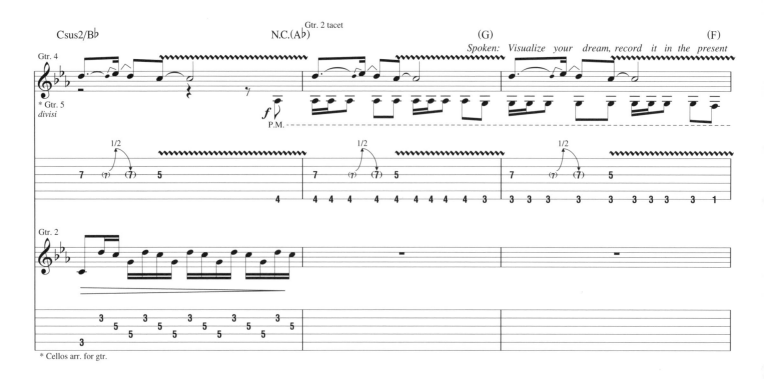

Spoken: Visualize your dream, record it in the present

* Cellos arr. for gtr.

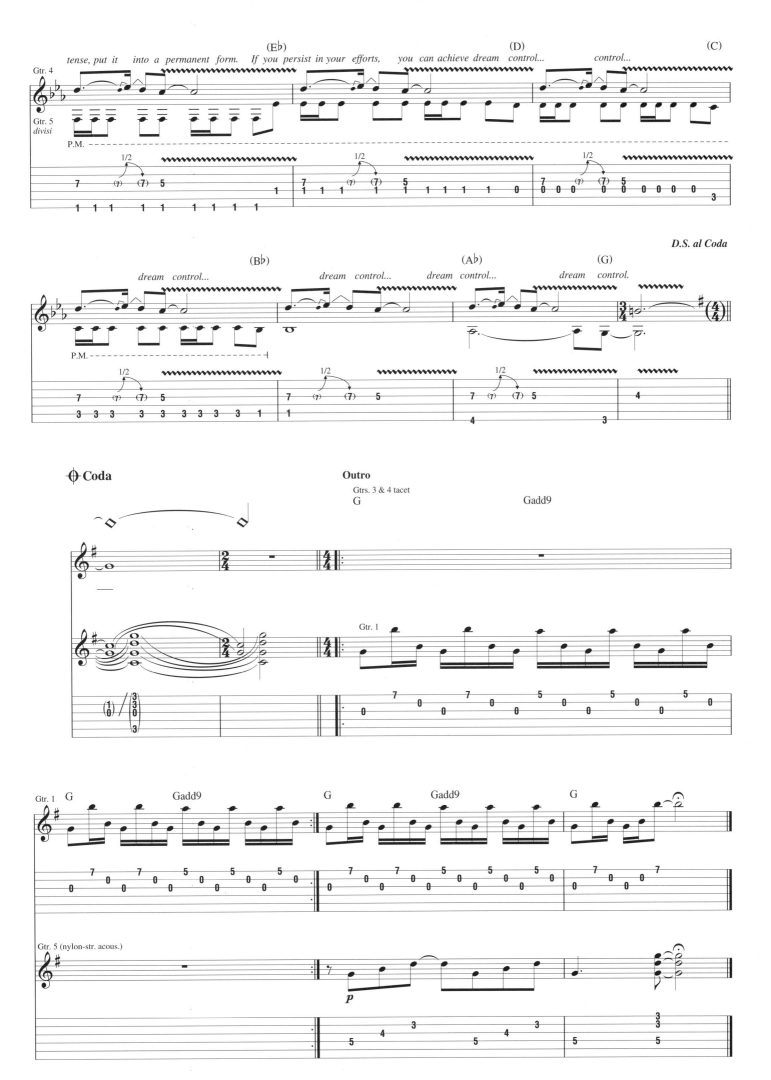

The Space Between

Words and Music by David J. Matthews and Glen Ballard

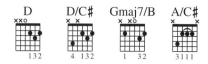

All gtrs.: Tune down 2 1/2 steps:
(low to high) B–E–A–D–F#–B

* Baritone gtr. arr. for standard gtr.; doubled throughout (music sounds a 4th lower than indicated).

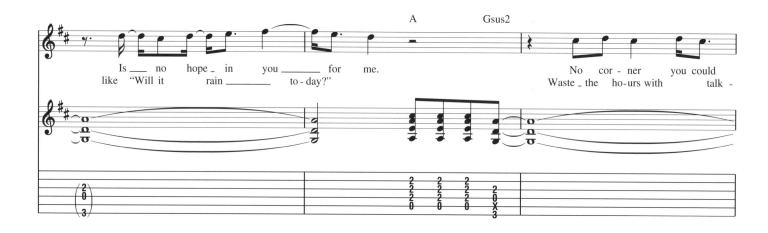

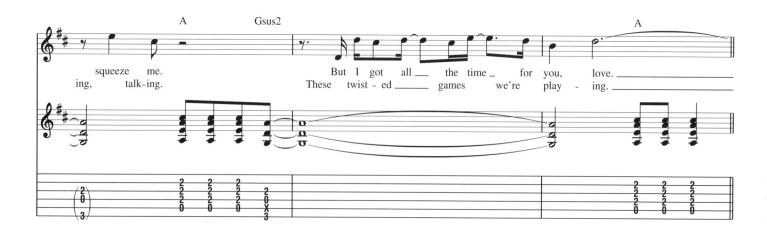

Bridge

Look at us spin-ning out in the mad - ness of a roll - er coast - er. ___ You know you went off like the dev-il in a

* Gtr. 4

Fill 1   **End Fill 1**

Gtr. 1

* Sax arr. for gtr.

Gtr. 4: w/ Fill 1

church, in the mid-dle of a crowd - ed ___ room.   All we can do,   my love,   is hope we don't take this ship down. ___

Gtr. 1

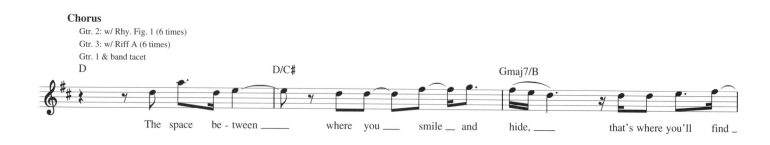

Chorus

Gtr. 2: w/ Rhy. Fig. 1 (6 times)
Gtr. 3: w/ Riff A (6 times)
Gtr. 1 & band tacet

The space be - tween ___ where you ___ smile ___ and hide, ___ that's where you'll find ___

(Band in)

___ me if I ___ get to go. ___ The space be - tween ___ the bul - lets in our fi -

Tears in Heaven

Words and Music by Eric Clapton and Will Jennings

have ya beg - gin' please, _____ beg - gin' please. _____

Interlude

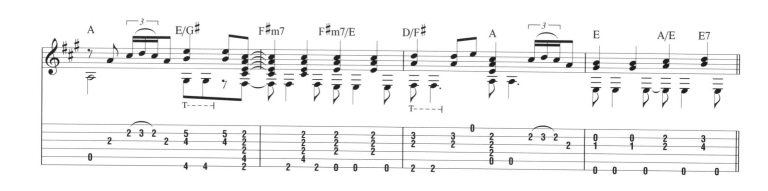

Chorus

Be - yond the door _____ there's peace, I'm sure, _____

214

D.S. al Coda
(take 1st lyrics)

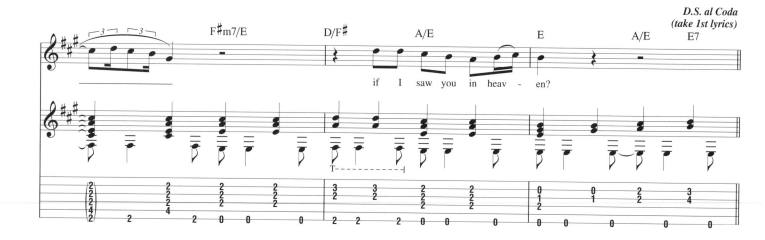

Coda

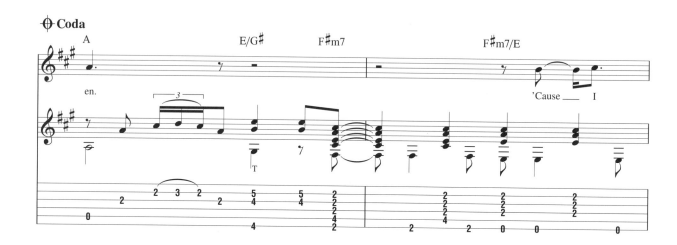

Thick as a Brick

Words and Music by Ian Anderson

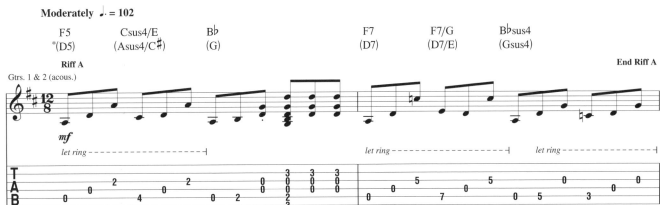

Gtrs. 1 & 2: Capo III

Intro

Moderately ♩. = 102

*Symbols in parentheses represent chord names respective to capoed guitar.
Symbols above reflect actual sounding chords. Capoed fret is "0" in tab.
Chord symbols reflect implied harmony.

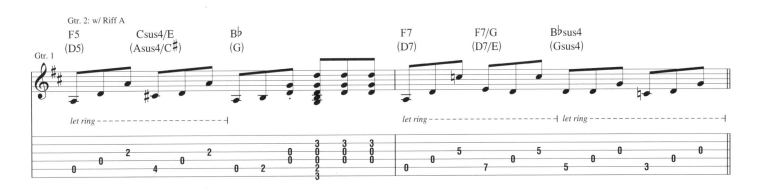

Verse

1. Real-ly don't mind _ if you sit this one _ out. _

**Gtr. 3

**Flute arr. for gtr.

***Gtrs. 1 & 2

***Composite arrangement

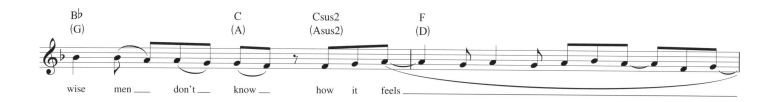

wise men ___ don't ___ know ___ how it feels ___

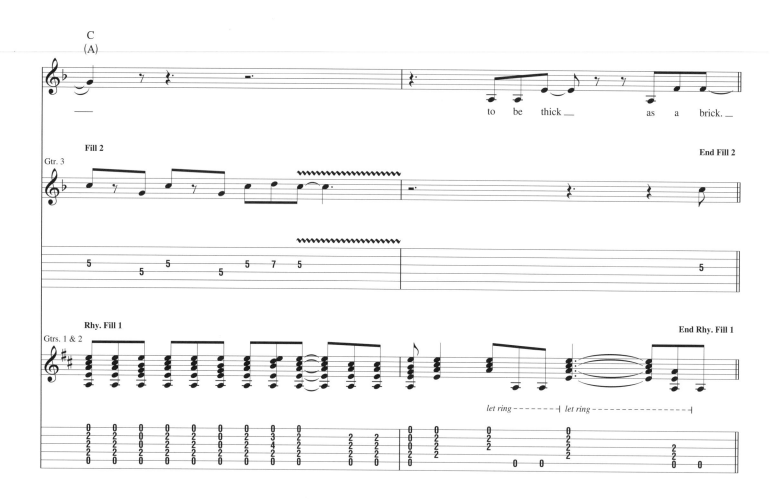

to be thick ___ as a brick. ___

Interlude

Chorus

Gtrs. 1 & 2: w/ Rhy. Fig. 1 (3 times)
Gtr. 3: w/ Riff E (3 times)

new shoes __ are worn __ at the heels, _____ and your

Riff H

Gtr. 4

End Riff H

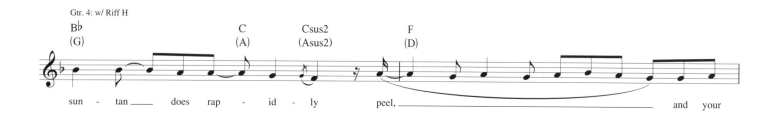

Gtr. 4: w/ Riff H

sun - tan __ does rap - id - ly peel, _____ and your

wise men __ don't __ know __ how it feels _____

Gtr. 4

Gtrs. 1 & 2: w/ Rhy. Fill 1
Gtr. 3: w/ Fill 2

Gtr. 4 tacet

__ to be thick as a brick. __

Interlude

Gtrs. 1 & 2: w/ Riff F
Gtr. 3: w/ Riff B (last 2 meas.)

Bridge

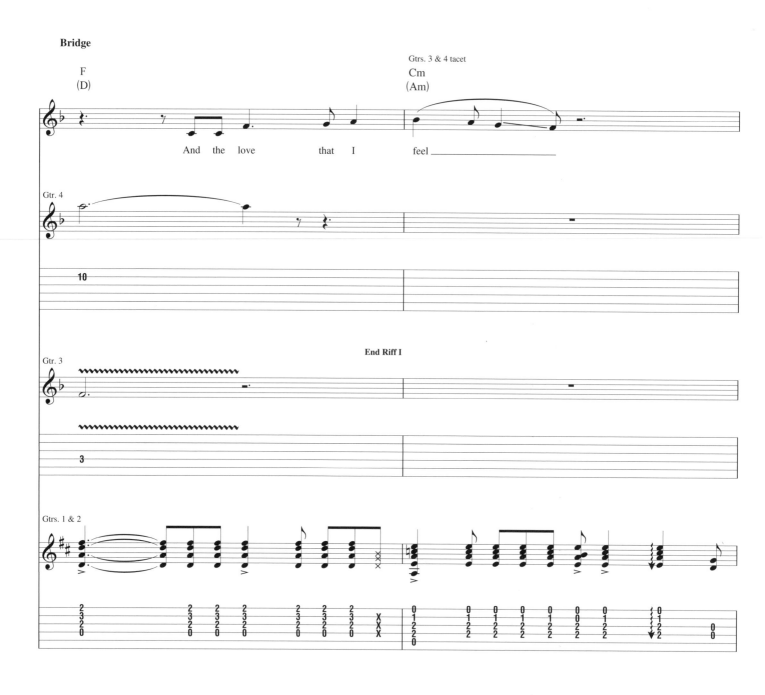

And the love   that I   feel

is   so   far   a - way.

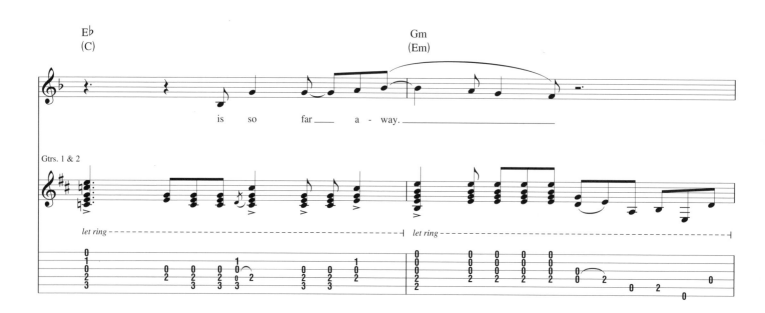

Outro

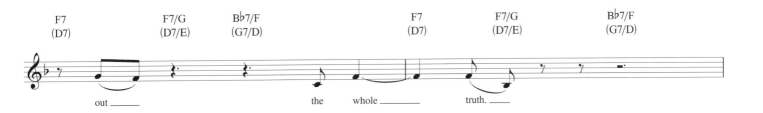

out _____ the whole _____ truth. _____

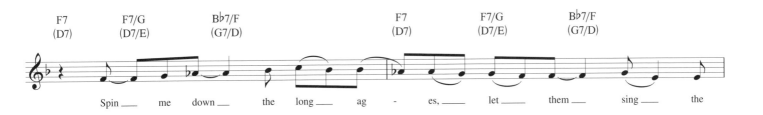

Spin ___ me down ___ the long ___ ag - es, ___ let ___ them ___ sing ___ the

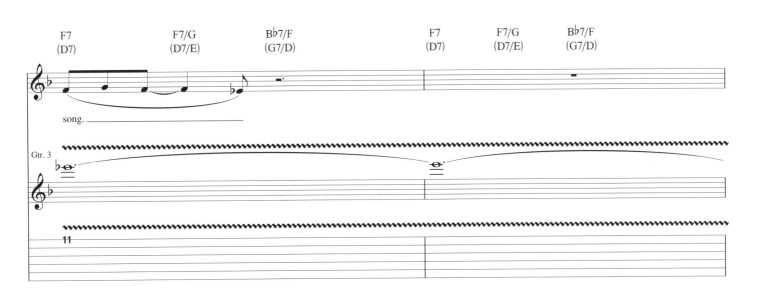

song. _____

Begin fade

Fade out

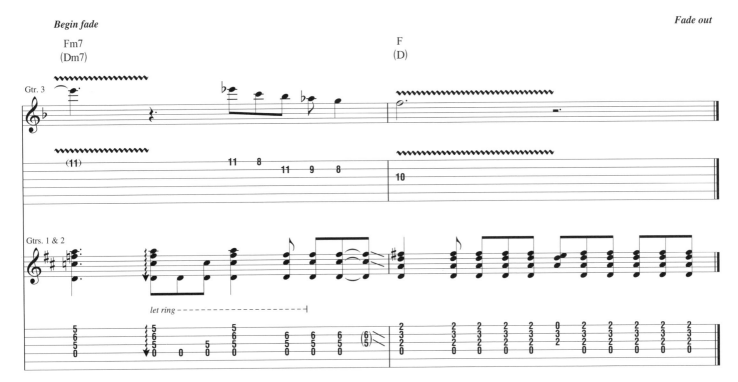

Upside Down

from the Universal Pictures and Imagine Entertainment film CURIOUS GEORGE

Words and Music by Jack Johnson

Uke tuning: A-D-F♯-B

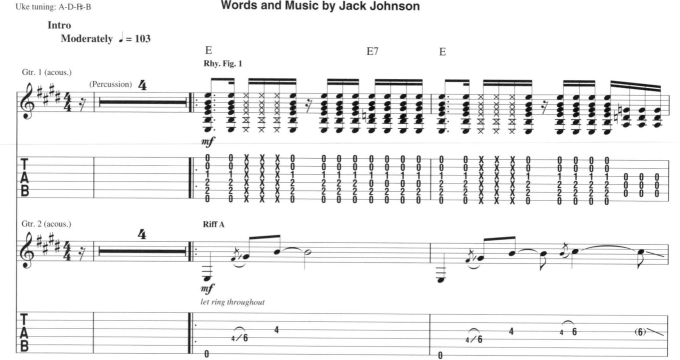

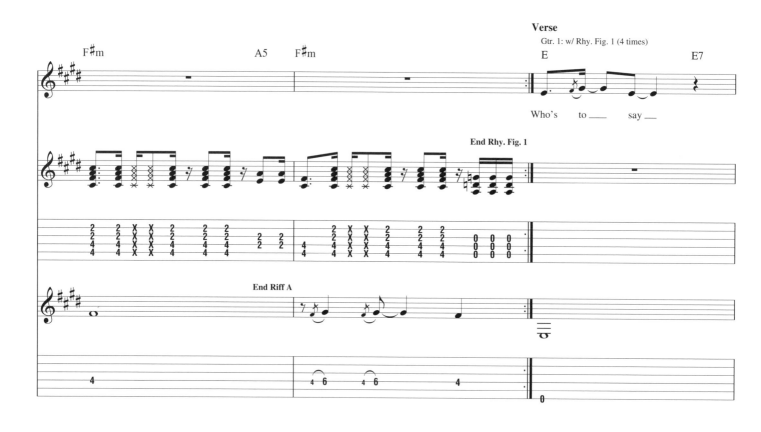

what's im - pos - si - ble? Well, they for - got ____ this world keeps spin - nin'. And ___ with

each new — day, — I can feel — a change — in ev - 'ry - thing. —

And as the sur - face breaks, re - flec - tions — fade, — but in some — ways — they re -

main the — same. — And as my mind — be - gins to spread its — wings, —

there's no stop - pin' cu - ri - os - i - ty. — I wan - na turn the whole thing

Chorus

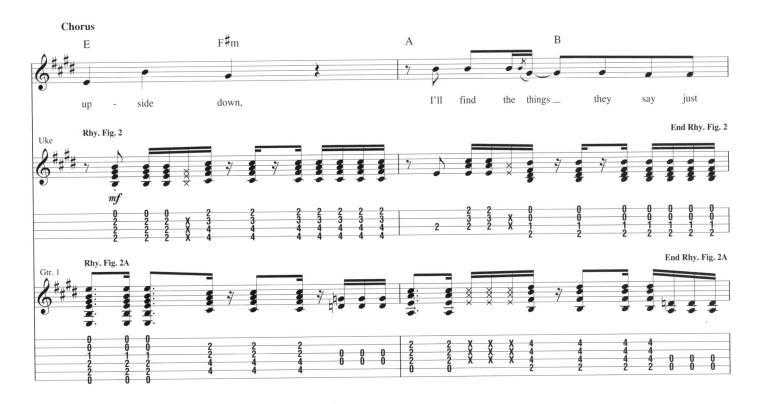

up - side down, I'll find the things — they say just

Uke: w/ Rhy. Fig. 2 (3 times)
Gtr. 1: w/ Rhy. Fig. 2A (3 times)

can't be — found. — I'll share this love — I find with ev - 'ry - one. —

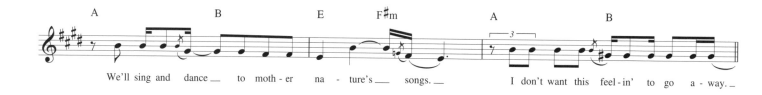

We'll sing and dance __ to moth-er na-ture's __ songs. __ I don't want this feel-in' to go a-way. __

Interlude

Gtr. 1: w/ Rhy. Fig. 1 (2 times)
Gtr. 2: w/ Riff A

Verse

Uke: w/ Rhy. Fig. 3
Gtr. 1: w/ Rhy. Fig. 1 (2 times)

2. Who's to ___ say ___

E   F#m   A5 F#m

I can't do ev - 'ry - thing? Well, I can __ try. __ And as I roll a - long __ I be -

E   E7   E   F#m   A5

gin to __ find __ things aren't al - ways just what they __ seem. __

Chorus

Uke: w/ Rhy. Fig. 2 (4 times)
Gtr. 1: w/ Rhy. Fig. 2A (4 times)

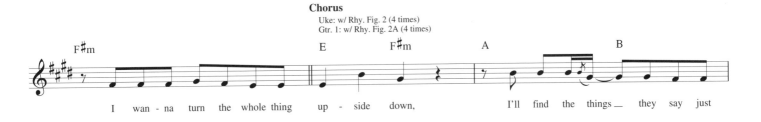

F#m   E   F#m   A   B

I wan - na turn the whole thing up - side down, I'll find the things __ they say just

E   F#m   A   B   E   F#m

can't be __ found. __ I'll share this love __ I find with ev - 'ry - one. __

A   B   E   F#m   A   B

We'll sing and dance __ to moth - er na - ture's __ songs. __ This world keeps spin - nin' and __ there's

Bridge

G#m   F#m

no   time   to waste. __   Well, it all __
(Oo, __

Uke

Gtr. 1

keeps spin - nin', spin - nin' 'round and 'round and

oo.)

Chorus

Uke: w/ Rhy. Fig. 2 (1 1/2 times)
Gtr. 1: w/ Rhy. Fig. 2A (1 1/2 times)

up - side down.   Who's to say what's im - pos - si - ble ___ and ___ can't be ___ found? ___

Outro

I don't want this feel - in' to go a - way. ___

 Uke

Gtr. 1

Gtr. 2

Please — don't go a - way. —

Please — don't go a - way. —

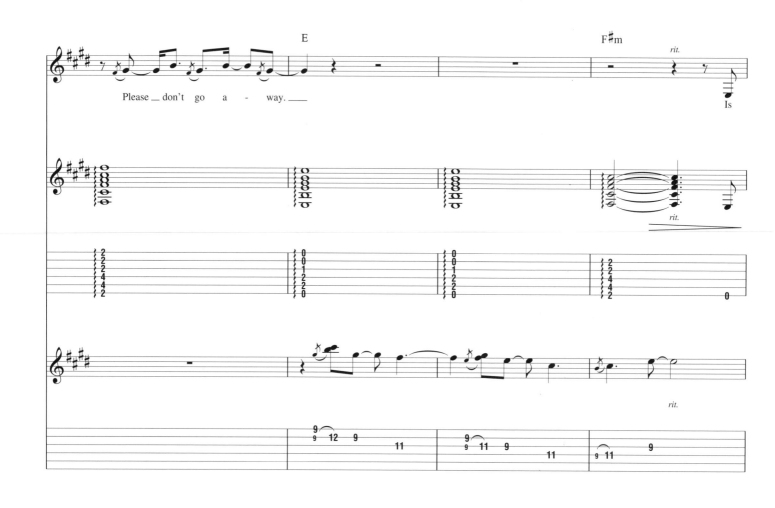

Please — don't go a - way. ___

E

F#m

Is

Slower ♩ = 84

A   F#m   E   F#m   A   E

this how it's sup - posed   to be? ___   Is   this how it's sup - posed   to be? ___

p

mp

Wanted Dead or Alive

Words and Music by Jon Bon Jovi and Richie Sambora

§ **Verse**

1. It's all the same,___ on - ly the names___ will change._____
   times I sleep,___ some-times it's not___ for days._____ The
   walk these streets,___ a load - ed six string on my back._____ I

Rhy. Fig. 1

*Play 3rd time only.
**Play simile 2nd & 3rd times.

Gtr. 1: w/ Fill 4, 2nd time   Gtr. 2: w/ Fill 2, 1st time

Ev - 'ry day ___ it seems we're wast-ing a - way. ___ An - oth - er place, ___ where the
peo-ple I meet al - ways go their sep-'rate ways. ___ Some-times you tell ___ the day ___ by the
play for keeps, ___ 'cause I might not make it back. ___ I've been ev - 'ry-where, ___ still I'm

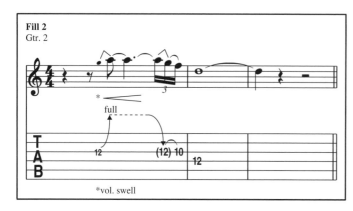

Fill 2
Gtr. 2

*vol. swell

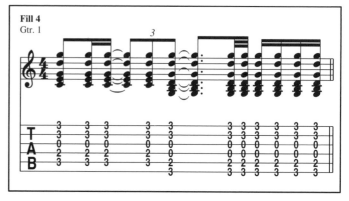

Fill 4
Gtr. 1

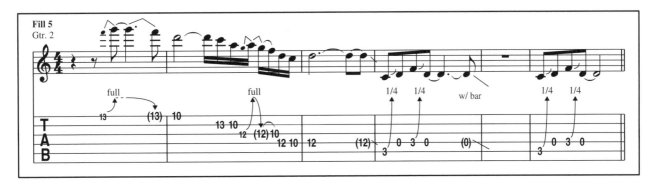

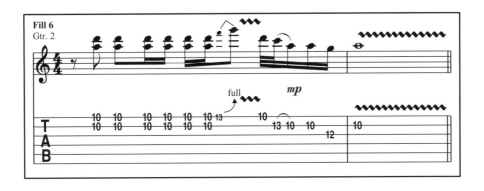

Chorus
Gtr. 1: w/ Rhy. Fig. 2, 1st 3 meas., simile
Gtr. 2 tacet

Oh, I'm a cow - boy, on a steel _ horse _ I ride. I'm

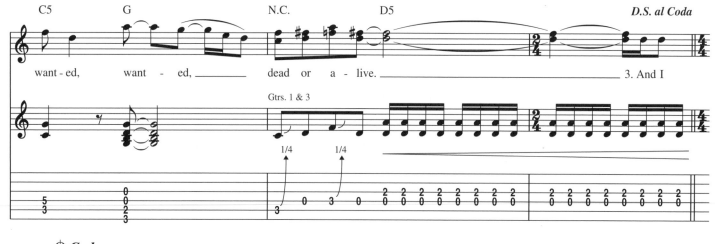

Coda

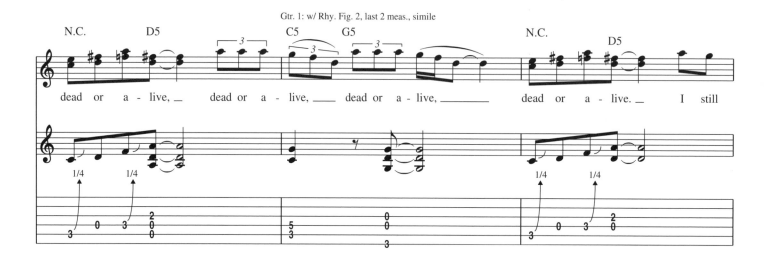

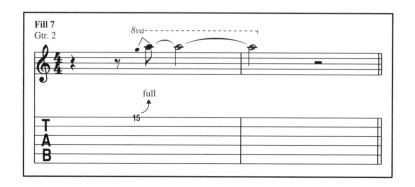

drive, __ I still drive, _____ dead or a - live, __ dead or a - live, _____

dead or a - live, __ dead or a - live, _____ dead or a - live. _____

Outro

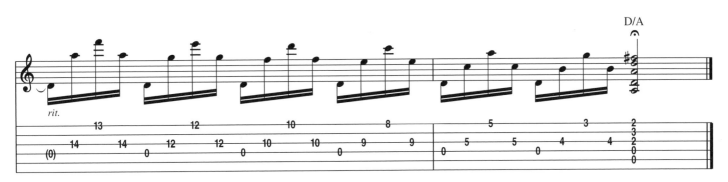

You've Got a Friend

Words and Music by Carole King

Gtr. 1: Capo III

Intro

Moderately ♩ = 94

*Symbols in parentheses represent chord names respective to capoed guitar.
Symbols above reflect actual sounding chord. Capoed fret is "0" in TAB.

Verse

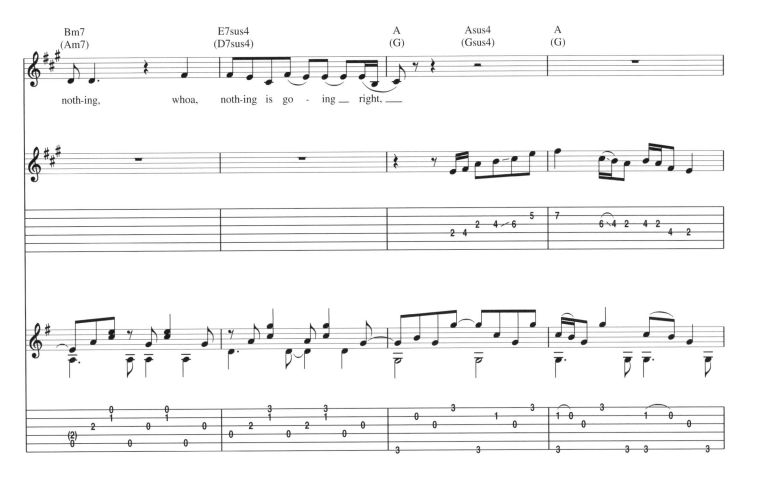

noth-ing, whoa, noth-ing is go - ing __ right, __

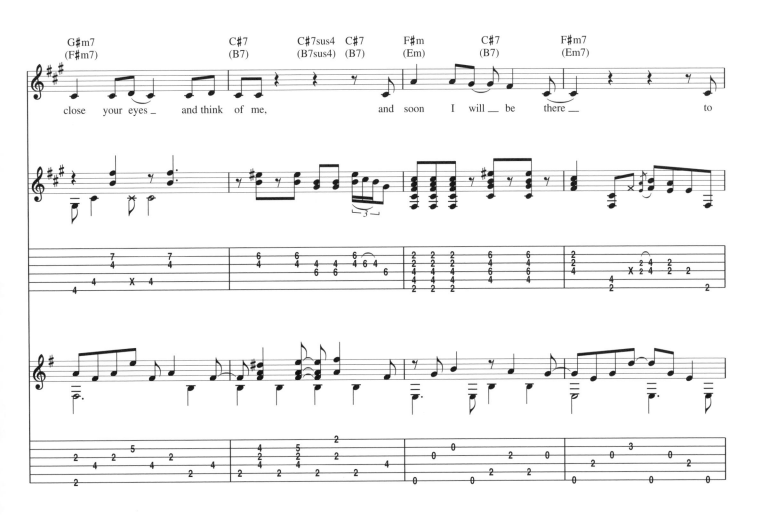

close your eyes __ and think of me, and soon I will __ be there __ to

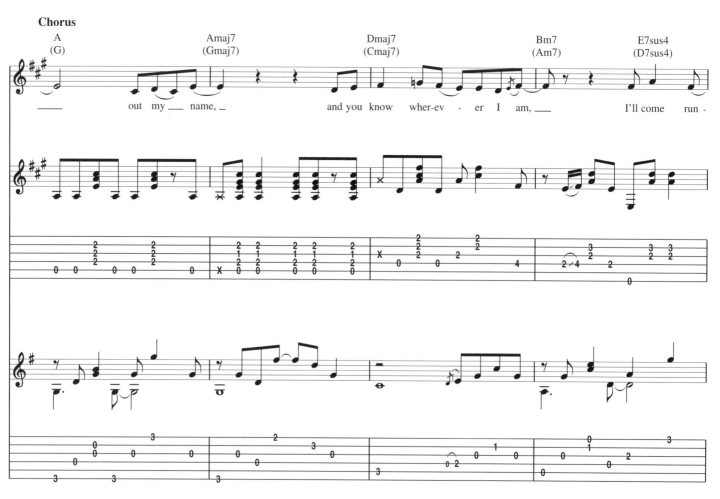

-ning, oh _ yeah, babe, _ to see you a - gain. _

Win-ter, spring, sum-mer or fall, _ now, all you got to do _ is _ call, _ and I'll

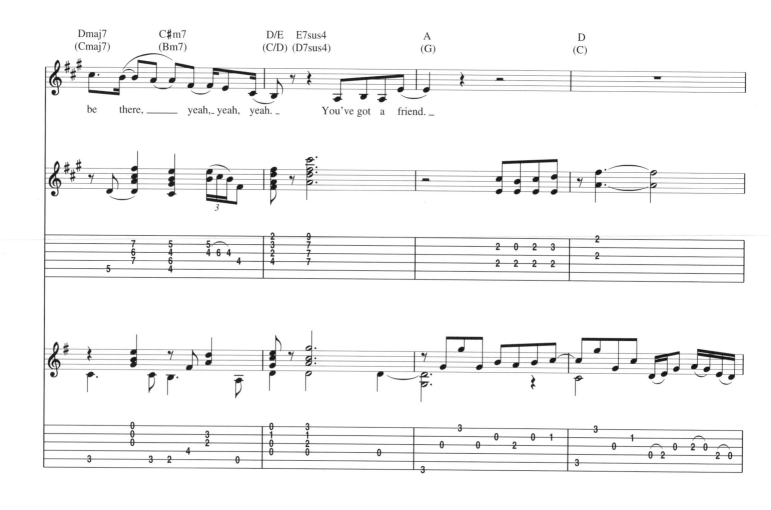

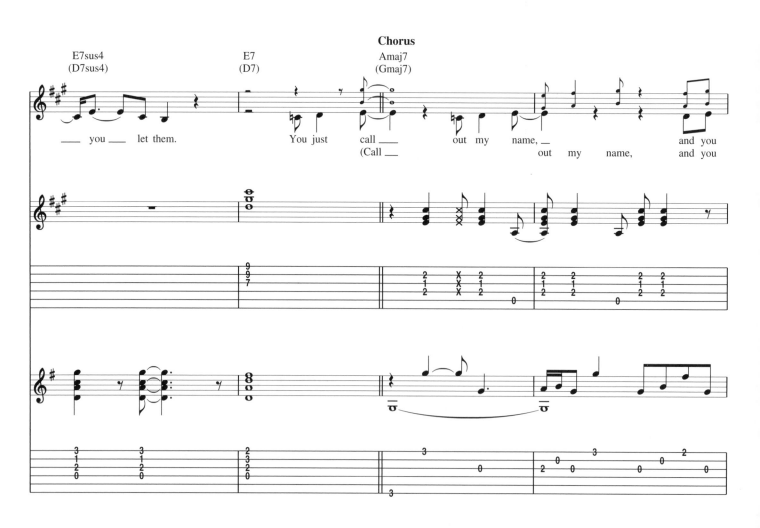

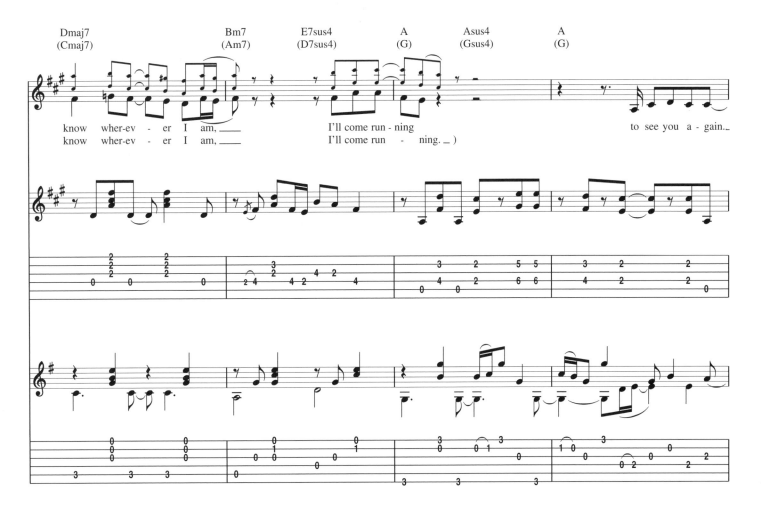

know wher-ev - er I am, ____ I'll come run - ning to see you a - gain._

know wher-ev - er I am, ____ I'll come run - ning. _)

_ Oh, babe, _ don't you know 'bout win-ter, spring, sum-mer or fall, _____ hey, now

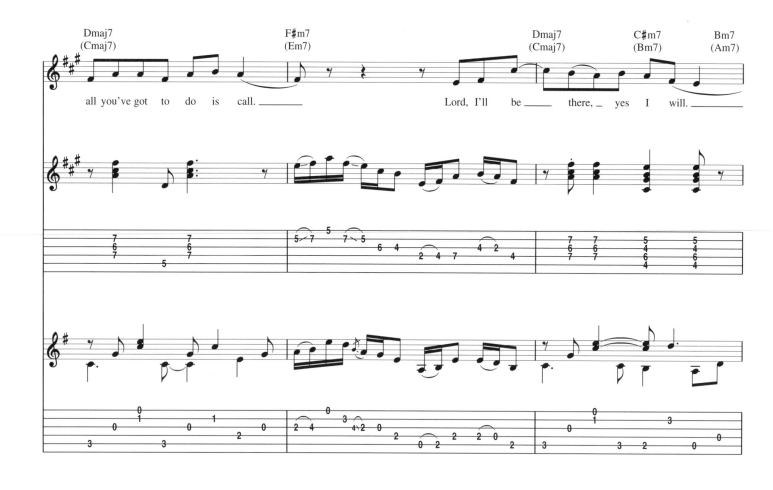

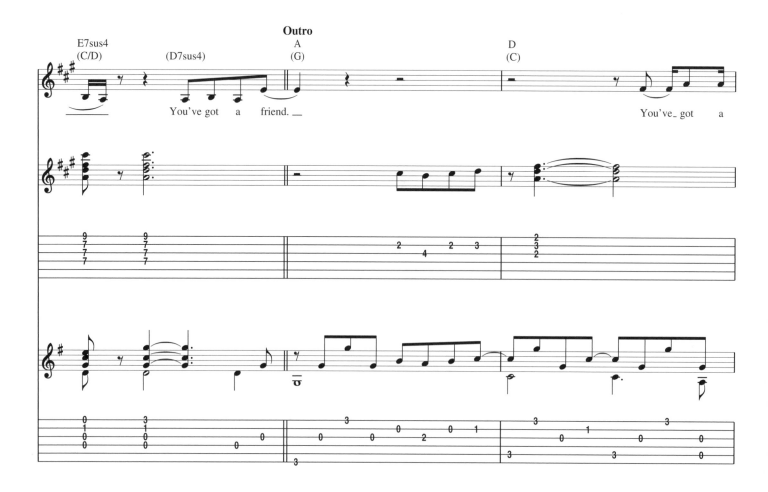

friend, _ yeah. _   Ain't it good_to know you've got ___ a friend?_   Ain't it good_ to know you've got a friend?_

___ _ yeah. _   Oh,   yeah, _ yeah. ___ You've got a friend. ___

Guitar Notation Legend

Guitar music can be notated three different ways: on a *musical staff*, in *tablature*, and in *rhythm slashes*.

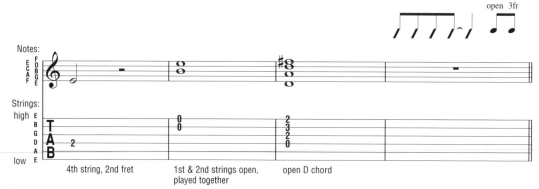

RHYTHM SLASHES are written above the staff. Strum chords in the rhythm indicated. Use the chord diagrams found at the top of the first page of the transcription for the appropriate chord voicings. Round noteheads indicate single notes.

THE MUSICAL STAFF shows pitches and rhythms and is divided by bar lines into measures. Pitches are named after the first seven letters of the alphabet.

TABLATURE graphically represents the guitar fingerboard. Each horizontal line represents a string, and each number represents a fret.

4th string, 2nd fret   1st & 2nd strings open, played together   open D chord

---

HALF-STEP BEND: Strike the note and bend up 1/2 step.

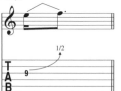

WHOLE-STEP BEND: Strike the note and bend up one step.

GRACE NOTE BEND: Strike the note and immediately bend up as indicated.

SLIGHT (MICROTONE) BEND: Strike the note and bend up 1/4 step.

BEND AND RELEASE: Strike the note and bend up as indicated, then release back to the original note. Only the first note is struck.

PRE-BEND: Bend the note as indicated, then strike it.

VIBRATO: The string is vibrated by rapidly bending and releasing the note with the fretting hand.

WIDE VIBRATO: The pitch is varied to a greater degree by vibrating with the fretting hand.

HAMMER-ON: Strike the first (lower) note with one finger, then sound the higher note (on the same string) with another finger by fretting it without picking.

PULL-OFF: Place both fingers on the notes to be sounded. Strike the first note and without picking, pull the finger off to sound the second (lower) note.

LEGATO SLIDE: Strike the first note and then slide the same fret-hand finger up or down to the second note. The second note is not struck.

SHIFT SLIDE: Same as legato slide, except the second note is struck.

TRILL: Very rapidly alternate between the notes indicated by continuously hammering on and pulling off.

TAPPING: Hammer ("tap") the fret indicated with the pick-hand index or middle finger and pull off to the note fretted by the fret hand.

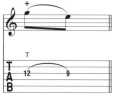

NATURAL HARMONIC: Strike the note while the fret-hand lightly touches the string directly over the fret indicated.

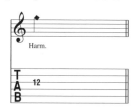

PINCH HARMONIC: The note is fretted normally and a harmonic is produced by adding the edge of the thumb or the tip of the index finger of the pick hand to the normal pick attack.

PICK SCRAPE: The edge of the pick is rubbed down (or up) the string, producing a scratchy sound.

MUFFLED STRINGS: A percussive sound is produced by laying the fret hand across the string(s) without depressing, and striking them with the pick hand.

PALM MUTING: The note is partially muted by the pick hand lightly touching the string(s) just before the bridge.

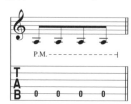

RAKE: Drag the pick across the strings indicated with a single motion.

TREMOLO PICKING: The note is picked as rapidly and continuously as possible.

VIBRATO BAR DIVE AND RETURN: The pitch of the note or chord is dropped a specified number of steps (in rhythm), then returned to the original pitch.

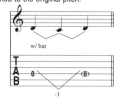

VIBRATO BAR SCOOP: Depress the bar just before striking the note, then quickly release the bar.

VIBRATO BAR DIP: Strike the note and then immediately drop a specified number of steps, then release back to the original pitch.

RECORDED VERSIONS®
The Best Note-For-Note Transcriptions Available

AUTHENTIC TRANSCRIPTIONS WITH NOTES AND TABLATURE

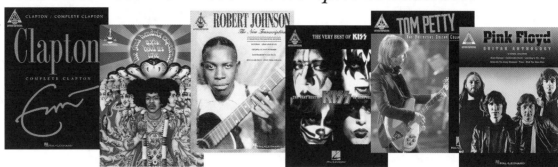

00690603	Aerosmith – O Yeah! Ultimate Hits ...	$27.99
00690178	Alice in Chains – Acoustic	$19.99
00694865	Alice in Chains – Dirt	$19.99
00694925	Alice in Chains – Jar of Flies/Sap.....	$19.99
00691091	Alice Cooper – Best of	$24.99
00690958	Duane Allman – Guitar Anthology	$29.99
00694932	Allman Brothers Band – Volume 1.....	$27.99
00694933	Allman Brothers Band – Volume 2.....	$24.99
00694934	Allman Brothers Band – Volume 3.....	$24.99
00690945	Alter Bridge – Blackbird	$24.99
00123558	Arctic Monkeys – AM	$24.99
00214869	Avenged Sevenfold – Best of 2005-2013	$24.99
00690489	Beatles – 1	$24.99
00694929	Beatles – 1962-1966	$24.99
00694930	Beatles – 1967-1970	$27.99
00694880	Beatles – Abbey Road	$19.99
00694832	Beatles – Acoustic Guitar................	$24.99
00690110	Beatles – White Album (Book 1)........	$19.99
00692385	Chuck Berry	$22.99
00147787	Black Crowes – Best of	$19.99
00690149	Black Sabbath	$17.99
00690901	Black Sabbath – Best of	$22.99
00691010	Black Sabbath – Heaven and Hell	$22.99
00690148	Black Sabbath – Master of Reality	$17.99
00690142	Black Sabbath – Paranoid	$16.99
00148544	Michael Bloomfield – Guitar Anthology	$24.99
00158600	Joe Bonamassa – Blues of Desperation	$22.99
00198117	Joe Bonamassa – Muddy Wolf at Red Rocks...............	$24.99
00283540	Joe Bonamassa – Redemption	$24.99
00690913	Boston	$19.99
00690491	David Bowie – Best of.....................	$19.99
00286503	Big Bill Broonzy – Guitar Collection ..	$19.99
00690261	The Carter Family Collection	$19.99
00691079	Johnny Cash – Best of	$22.99
00690936	Eric Clapton – Complete Clapton	$29.99
00694869	Eric Clapton – Unplugged	$24.99
00124873	Eric Clapton – Unplugged (Deluxe) ...	$27.99
00138731	Eric Clapton & Friends – The Breeze	$22.99
00139967	Coheed & Cambria – In Keeping Secrets of Silent Earth: 3	$24.99
00141704	Jesse Cook – Works, Vol. 1	$19.99
00288787	Creed – Greatest Hits.....................	$22.99
00690819	Creedence Clearwater Revival	$24.99
00690648	Jim Croce – Very Best of..................	$19.99
00690572	Steve Cropper – Soul Man	$19.99
00690613	Crosby, Stills & Nash – Best of........	$27.99
00690784	Def Leppard – Best of	$22.99
00695831	Derek and the Dominos – Layla & Other Assorted Love Songs ..	$24.99
00291164	Dream Theater – Distance Over Time	$24.99
00278631	Eagles – Greatest Hits 1971-1975	$22.99
00278632	Eagles – Very Best of	$34.99
00690515	Extreme II – Pornograffiti................	$24.99
00150257	John Fahey – Guitar Anthology	$19.99
00690664	Fleetwood Mac – Best of.................	$24.99
00691024	Foo Fighters – Greatest Hits	$22.99
00120220	Robben Ford – Guitar Anthology	$29.99
00295410	Rory Gallagher – Blues	$24.99
00139460	Grateful Dead – Guitar Anthology......	$24.99

00691190	Peter Green – Best of......................	$24.99
00287517	Greta Van Fleet – Anthem of the Peaceful Army	$19.99
00287515	Greta Van Fleet – From the Fires	$19.99
00694798	George Harrison – Anthology............	$22.99
00692930	Jimi Hendrix – Are You Experienced?	$27.99
00692931	Jimi Hendrix – Axis: Bold As Love.....	$24.99
00690304	Jimi Hendrix – Band of Gypsys	$24.99
00694944	Jimi Hendrix – Blues.......................	$27.99
00692932	Jimi Hendrix – Electric Ladyland.......	$27.99
00660029	Buddy Holly – Best of	$22.99
00200446	Iron Maiden – Guitar Tab	$29.99
00694912	Eric Johnson – Ah Via Musicom	$24.99
00690271	Robert Johnson – Transcriptions.......	$24.99
00690427	Judas Priest – Best of	$24.99
00690492	B.B. King – Anthology.....................	$24.99
00130447	B.B. King – Live at the Regal	$19.99
00690134	Freddie King – Collection	$19.99
00327968	Marcus King – El Dorado	$22.99
00690157	Kiss – Alive	$19.99
00690356	Kiss – Alive II	$22.99
00291163	Kiss – Very Best of	$22.99
00690377	Kris Kristofferson – Guitar Collection	$19.99
00690834	Lamb of God – Ashes of the Wake	$24.99
00690525	George Lynch – Best of	$24.99
00690955	Lynyrd Skynyrd – All-Time Greatest Hits	$24.99
00694954	Lynyrd Skynyrd – New Best of	$24.99
00690577	Yngwie Malmsteen – Anthology	$29.99
00694896	John Mayall with Eric Clapton – Blues Breakers	$19.99
00694952	Megadeth – Countdown to Extinction	$24.99
00276065	Megadeth – Greatest Hits: Back to the Start	$24.99
00694951	Megadeth – Rust in Peace................	$24.99
00690011	Megadeth – Youthanasia..................	$24.99
00209876	Metallica – Hardwired to Self-Destruct	$22.99
00690646	Pat Metheny – One Quiet Night	$22.99
00102591	Wes Montgomery – Guitar Anthology	$24.99
00691092	Gary Moore – Best of	$24.99
00694802	Gary Moore – Still Got the Blues	$24.99
00355456	Alanis Morisette – Jagged Little Pill	$22.99
00690611	Nirvana...	$22.95
00694913	Nirvana – In Utero	$19.99
00694883	Nirvana – Nevermind	$19.99
00690026	Nirvana – Unplugged in New York.....	$19.99
00265439	Nothing More – Tab Collection	$24.99
00243349	Opeth – Best of	$22.99
00690499	Tom Petty – Definitive Guitar Collection	$19.99
00121933	Pink Floyd – Acoustic Guitar Collection	$24.99
00690428	Pink Floyd – Dark Side of the Moon ..	$19.99
00244637	Pink Floyd – Guitar Anthology..........	$24.99
00239799	Pink Floyd – The Wall	$24.99
00690789	Poison – Best of	$19.99
00690625	Prince – Very Best of......................	$22.99
00690003	Queen – Classic Queen	$24.99
00694975	Queen – Greatest Hits.....................	$25.99
00694910	Rage Against the Machine	$22.99
00119834	Rage Against the Machine – Guitar Anthology	$24.99

00690426	Ratt – Best of................................	$19.95
00690055	Red Hot Chili Peppers – Blood Sugar Sex Magik.....................	$19.99
00690379	Red Hot Chili Peppers – Californication...............................	$19.99
00690673	Red Hot Chili Peppers – Greatest Hits	$22.99
00690852	Red Hot Chili Peppers – Stadium Arcadium	$27.99
00690511	Django Reinhardt – Definitive Collection	$22.99
00690014	Rolling Stones – Exile on Main Street	$24.99
00690631	Rolling Stones – Guitar Anthology	$29.99
00323854	Rush – The Spirit of Radio: Greatest Hits, 1974-1987..................	$22.99
00173534	Santana – Guitar Anthology..............	$27.99
00276350	Joe Satriani – What Happens Next ...	$24.99
00690566	Scorpions – Best of	$24.99
00690604	Bob Seger – Guitar Collection	$24.99
00234543	Ed Sheeran – Divide*	$19.99
00691114	Slash – Guitar Anthology	$29.99
00690813	Slayer – Guitar Collection	$19.99
00690419	Slipknot	$19.99
00316982	Smashing Pumpkins – Greatest Hits	$22.99
00690912	Soundgarden – Guitar Anthology.......	$24.99
00120004	Steely Dan – Best of.......................	$24.99
00120081	Sublime	$19.99
00690531	System of a Down – Toxicity.............	$19.99
00694824	James Taylor – Best of	$19.99
00694887	Thin Lizzy – Best of	$19.99
00253237	Trivium – Guitar Tab Anthology........	$24.99
00690683	Robin Trower – Bridge of Sighs........	$19.99
00156024	Steve Vai – Guitar Anthology............	$34.99
00660137	Steve Vai – Passion & Warfare	$27.50
00295076	Van Halen – 30 Classics	$29.99
00690024	Stevie Ray Vaughan – Couldn't Stand the Weather...............	$19.99
00660058	Stevie Ray Vaughan – Lightnin' Blues 1983-1987.................	$29.99
00217455	Stevie Ray Vaughan – Plays Slow Blues............................	$19.99
00694835	Stevie Ray Vaughan – The Sky Is Crying	$24.99
00690015	Stevie Ray Vaughan – Texas Flood ...	$19.99
00694789	Muddy Waters – Deep Blues.............	$24.99
00152161	Doc Watson – Guitar Anthology	$22.99
00690071	Weezer (The Blue Album)	$19.99
00117511	Whitesnake – Guitar Collection	$22.99
00122303	Yes – Guitar Collection	$22.99
00690443	Frank Zappa – Hot Rats	$22.99
00121684	ZZ Top – Early Classics...................	$27.99
00690589	ZZ Top – Guitar Anthology	$24.99

COMPLETE SERIES LIST ONLINE!

HAL•LEONARD®
www.halleonard.com

Prices and availability subject to change without notice.
*Tab transcriptions only.

0720
272

GUITAR BIBLES

from  HAL•LEONARD®

Hal Leonard proudly presents the Guitar Bible series. Each volume contains great songs in authentic, note-for-note transcriptions with lyrics and tablature.

ACOUSTIC GUITAR BIBLE

35 acoustic classics: Angie • Building a Mystery • Change the World • Dust in the Wind • Hold My Hand • Iris • Maggie May • Southern Cross • Tears in Heaven • Wild World • and more.
00690432..$24.99

ACOUSTIC HITS GUITAR BIBLE

34 must-have acoustic tunes: Baby, I Love Your Way • Can't Buy Me Love • Daydream • Fast Car • Jack and Diane • Landslide • Mrs. Robinson • More Than a Feeling • Peace Train • Sparks • Used to Love Her • Walk on the Wild Side • Working Class Hero • You Don't Mess Around with Jim • and more.
00691094..$19.99

BLUES GUITAR BIBLE

35 blues tunes: Boom Boom • Hide Away • I Can't Quit You Baby • I'm Your Hoochie Coochie Man • Killing Floor • Pride and Joy • Sweet Little Angel • The Thrill Is Gone • and more.
00690437..$24.99

BLUES-ROCK GUITAR BIBLE

35 songs: Cross Road Blues (Crossroads) • Hide Away • The House Is Rockin' • Love Struck Baby • Move It On Over • Piece of My Heart • Statesboro Blues • You Shook Me • more.
00690450..$19.95

CLASSIC ROCK GUITAR BIBLE

33 essential rock songs: Beast of Burden • Cat Scratch Fever • Double Vision • Free Ride • Hard to Handle • Life in the Fast Lane • The Stroke • Won't Get Fooled Again • and more.
00690662..$24.99

DISCO GUITAR BIBLE

30 stand-out songs from the disco days: Brick House • Disco Inferno • Funkytown • Get Down Tonight • I Love the Night Life • Le Freak • Stayin' Alive • Y.M.C.A. • and more.
00690627..$19.99

FINGERPICKING GUITAR BIBLE

30 favorites, including: America • Anji • Blackbird • The Boxer • Classical Gas • Cross Road Blues • Drifting • Dust in the Wind • Helplessly Hoping • Jack Fig • Julia • Little Martha • Mister Sandman • Morning Is the Long Way Home • Song for George • Tears in Heaven • Time in a Bottle • and more.
00691040..$19.99

GRUNGE GUITAR BIBLE

30 songs: All Apologies • Counting Blue Cars • Glycerine • Jesus Christ Pose • Lithium • Man in the Box • Nearly Lost You • Smells like Teen Spirit • This Is a Call • Violet • and more.
00690649..$24.99

HARD ROCK GUITAR BIBLE

35 songs: Ballroom Blitz • Bang a Gong • Barracuda • Living After Midnight • Rock You like a Hurricane • School's Out • Welcome to the Jungle • You Give Love a Bad Name • more.
00690453..$22.99

JAZZ GUITAR BIBLE

31 songs: Body and Soul • In a Sentimental Mood • My Funny Valentine • Nuages • Satin Doll • So What • Star Dust • Take Five • Tangerine • Yardbird Suite • and more.
00690466..$24.99

PROGRESSIVE ROCK GUITAR BIBLE

28 great art-rock and metal tunes: Astronomy Domine • Empire • Eyes of a Stranger • Ghost of Karelia • Lavender • Lucky Man • Money • Monument • Rhythm of Love • The Story in Your Eyes • Strange Magic • Turn It On Again • 21st Century Schizoid Man • The Wall • and more.
00690626..$19.99

R&B GUITAR BIBLE

35 R&B classics: Brick House • Fire • I Got You (I Feel Good) • Love Rollercoaster • Shining Star • Sir Duke • Super Freak • and more.
00690452..$19.95

ROCK BASS BIBLE

35 rock bass hits: Another One Bites the Dust • Come Together • Fat Bottomed Girls • I Want You to Want Me • Miss You • Suffragette City • Sweet Emotion • White Room • You Shook Me • more!
00690446..$19.99

ROCK GUITAR BIBLE

33 songs: All Day and All of the Night • Born to Be Wild • Day Tripper • Hey Joe • Jailhouse Rock • Money • Paranoid • Sultans of Swing • Walk This Way • You Really Got Me • more!
00690313..$22.99

ROCKABILLY GUITAR BIBLE

31 songs from artists such as Elvis, Buddy Holly and the Brian Setzer Orchestra: Blue Suede Shoes • Hello Mary Lou • Peggy Sue • Rock This Town • Travelin' Man • and more.
00690570..$22.99

SOUTHERN ROCK GUITAR BIBLE

25 southern rock classics: Can't You See • Free Bird • Hold On Loosely • La Grange • Midnight Rider • Sweet Home Alabama • and more.
00690723..$22.99

Prices, contents, and availability subject to change without notice.
For more information, see your local music dealer, or write to:

 HAL•LEONARD®